Your First Year As
PRINCIPAL

Everything You Need to Know That They Don't Teach You in School

Revised 2nd Edition

By Tena Green

D1166773

YOUR FIRST YEAR AS PRINCIPAL: EVERYTHING YOU NEED TO KNOW THAT THEY DON'T TEACH YOU IN SCHOOL REVISED 2ND EDITION

Library of Congress Cataloging-in-Publication Data

Green, Tena, 1960-

Your first year as principal : everything you need to know that they don't teach you in school / by Tena Green. -- Rev. 2nd ed.

p. cm.

Includes bibliographical references and index.

ISBN-13: 978-1-60138-624-3 (alk. paper)

ISBN-10: 1-60138-624-9 (alk. paper)

1. First year school principals--United States--Handbooks, manuals, etc. 2. School management and organization--United States--Handbooks, manuals, etc. I. Title.

LB2831.92.K45 2010

371.2'012--dc22

2010010848

Printed in the United States

Printed on Recycled Paper

PROJECT MANAGER: Shannon McCarthy • smccarthy@atlantic-pub.com
PROOFREADER: C&P Marse • bluemoon6749@bellsouth.net
FRONT & BACK COVER DESIGN: Jackie Miller • millerjackiej@gmail.com

Reduce. Reuse. RECYCLE.

A decade ago, Atlantic Publishing signed the Green Press Initiative. These guidelines promote environmentally friendly practices, such as using recycled stock and vegetable-based inks, avoiding waste, choosing energy-efficient resources, and promoting a no-pulping policy. We now use 100-percent recycled stock on all our books. The results: in one year, switching to post-consumer recycled stock saved 24 mature trees, 5,000 gallons of water, the equivalent of the total energy used for one home in a year, and the equivalent of the greenhouse gases from one car driven for a year.

Over the years, we have adopted a number of dogs from rescues and shelters. First there was Bear and after he passed, Ginger and Scout. Now, we have Kira, another rescue. They have brought immense joy and love not just into our lives, but into the lives of all who met them.

We want you to know a portion of the profits of this book will be donated in Bear, Ginger and Scout's memory to local animal shelters, parks, conservation organizations, and other individuals and nonprofit organizations in need of assistance.

– Douglas & Sherri Brown,
President & Vice-President of Atlantic Publishing

DEDICATION

This book is dedicated to all the great principals who contributed to this effort, without whom this book would not be possible; to Bill Hall and Dr. Richard DiPatri; and especially to the great principals who left a lasting impression on my life, Mr. Carl Howard and Mr. Bruce Kimbrell.

CONTENTS

Chapter 2: The Gap Analysis 55

Chapter 3: The Standards 77

Chapter 6: Your Teachers 143

Chapter 7: Your Students 163

Chapter 8: The Parents 185

Chapter 9: Focusing on You 197

CAST OF CHARACTERS

In the course of reading this book, you will notice quotes from many principals who have been kind enough to lend their insights to help you, the first-year principal. Below you will find a list of each of these excellent school leaders and a brief introduction.

Former First-Year Principals

The following individuals were hired as first-year principals to begin the 2007-2008 academic year. The interviews were conducted following the first year of each individual's principalship.

- **Tammy Brown** is the principal at Sabal Palm Elementary School in Naples, Florida.

- **Katherine Munn** is the principal at Littlewood Elementary School in Gainesville, Florida.

- **Tret Witherspoon** is the principal at Taliaferro County Charter School in Crawford, Georgia.

Veteran Principals and Exceptional Leaders

These are the experts: principals and school leaders of varying levels of experience, all of whom have vast knowledge and invaluable insights who were kind enough to share for the purposes of this book.

- **Roy Miller** is a six-year principal at Mooreland Heights Elementary School in Knoxville, Tennessee.

- **Barbara A. Belanger** is a six-year principal at Harbor City Elementary in Melbourne, Florida.

- **Pamela C. Mitchell** is a six-year principal at Central Middle School in West Melbourne, Florida.

- **Jory Westberry** is an eight-year principal at Tommie Barfield Elementary on Marco Island, Florida.

- **Michael D. Miller** is a ten-year principal at Saturn Elementary School in Cocoa, Florida.

- **Oliver Phipps** is an 11-year principal at Estates Elementary School in Naples, Florida.

- **Dr. Nancy J. Graham** is a 14-year principal at Naples High School in Naples, Florida.

- **Barry Pichard** is a 16-year principal at Sunrise Elementary School in Palm Bay, Florida.

- **Robert Spano** is a 17-year principal at Mike Davis Elementary School in Naples, Florida.

- **Dr. Leonard I. Weiss** is a 21-year principal at the A. Quinn Jones Center in Gainesville, Florida.

- **Dr. James A. Gasparino** is a 22-year principal at Pelican Marsh Elementary School in Naples, Florida.

- **John Fielding** is a 22-year principal at Idylwild Elementary School in Gainesville, Florida.

- **Dr. Chet Sanders** is a 26-year principal at the Professional Academies Magnet at Loften High School in Gainesville, Florida.

- **John Redd** is the principal at Bellevue Junior High School in Bellevue, Ohio.

- **Bill Hall** is the director of Educational Leadership and Professional Development for the Brevard County School District in Florida.

- **Dr. Richard A. DiPatri** is the superintendent of Schools for Penn Foster Virtual High School and the former superintendent for the Brevard County School District in Florida.

FOREWORD

I remember walking into "my" building my first day as a new principal. I had spent many years as an educator in the public schools of New York City, both as a teacher and as an assistant principal, but this was different. After a rigorous interview process, and after waiting for an entire summer, I was informed that I had been selected for the position.

I walked into an office and was greeted not by a secretary, but a fax machine working overtime, spewing out reams of paper from both the superintendent's office and the central board of education. I spent the day reading through the memos and directives and opening the mail that had accumulated over the summer.

The next day, I met the faculty. They were a group of educators who looked upon me as the "enemy" because they had an allegiance to another person in the school who did not get the position. Could I win them over? The students were to enter the building the next day, and it seemed like nothing was ready. Was the curriculum in place? Were student programs ready? Were all of the teachers hired and given their proper assignments? Were the classrooms inviting? Was the support staff in place? What about new students who needed to be enrolled at the school? How should I respond to the fax machine that did not quit?

In all the classes I took while studying to become an administrator, there was nothing taught that could have prepared me for the experiences I had during the first weeks and months of being a new principal.

Did I survive? I am happy to say yes. Could my life have been easier if I had some preliminary guidelines to help me through those hectic beginnings? Absolutely.

It is with these memories in place that I am happy to recommend Tena Green's book, *Your First Year as a Principal: Everything You Need to Know That They Don't Teach You in School.*

This is a wonderful book written by someone examining a principal's job not as an educator, but from the unique view of someone who has been in schools in a variety of roles, working with teachers, students, and administrators.

Newly appointed principals enter into their positions with a vision of where they want their school to be in a few years, building on past strengths and eliminating any areas of concern. The chapters in this book are presented in a clear and concise way that will assist a new principal in achieving these goals.

As the head administrator of a school, what are your priorities? Hopefully, your main priority will be the students in your building. Everything you do should fall under the heading, "Is this good for my students?" Can your students answer the following questions: What am I learning? Why am I learning this? How can I use it?

Although the best interest of our students is the first priority, how do we deal with the myriad other responsibilities that we, as principals, incur?

The principal is a master juggler. As a principal, you know you have to deal with students, faculty, guidance counselors, school aides, secretaries, and building support teams, such as custodial and cafeteria workers and the school nurse; however, the job does not end inside the school walls. The principal is also an integral part of the community — dealing with parents, civic organizations, local businesses, and cultural institutions, just to name a few. There are also demands from the district superintendent, the local school board, and the state and federal government departments of education. How does one balance the needs of the position with the need for a personal life?

This book will give newly appointed principals, and even those who have been in the position longer, valuable insight into the difficult, but ultimately rewarding, job of a school leader.

The chapters inform the reader about a variety of important issues confronting new principals. They detail a principal's responsibilities, how to assess what needs to be done in the school, how to implement change effectively, and how to insure that change becomes institutionalized. The book also contains insightful commentary from successful principals in the form of case studies. Thoughtful and topical questions are posed and answered in a way that provides valuable tools for the novice school leader.

Best of luck to you as you embark on your new journey. Your position is an important one that can potentially have a profound effect on your school, community, and most important, your students. Keep this book with you and refer to it often throughout your years as a school leader, as it is a valuable resource.

Ira Shankman, B.S., M.A., M.Ed.
Music and Performing Arts Professions
New York University

INTRODUCTION

Besides my father, there was one other man who had a remarkable impact on my life, and that was my principal, Carl Howard. Mr. Howard was a big man, his size alone intimidating, but more important, he was a man who left a lasting impression on me. When asked why he made such an impact, I realized there was not one reason, but many. It was not just his gentle nature, his kindness, or his firm, yet understanding, authority; it was also his ability to laugh with students and faculty, his fairness in discipline, his obvious regret when having to use that discipline, and his sincere affection for the school. All of these qualities made my school years an everlasting memory, and it was due to one great man.

As a student, there was never a thought given to what my principal's duties were. As a parent, my focus was on my children's education, not on the principal's responsibility for that education. It was when I worked as a teacher's assistant, intervention specialist, and substitute secretary that I caught a mere glimpse of the enormous undertaking a principal's job entails. Looking back on the 30-plus years of these different perspectives at work, witnessing the importance of a principal's job and its necessity was an eye-opening experience. It was also the reason I decided to try to help first-year principals as they struggled to define their places as leaders. My experience comes from many different vantage points, and I have tremendous respect for principals and the challenges they face.

The realization of my principal's impact on students and learning more of what is expected of today's principals gave me reason to wonder what it is like to carry such weight, especially for new principals entering their first year.

I have learned that a good principal's main objective is to meet the needs of his or her students, diverse as the lot may be — to guide them, help them, discipline them, or encourage them, no matter what the situation. A worthy leader brings all his or her talents, not just to the office, but to every hallway and room of the school. Students will love and respect you for it, and you will be a leader who makes a difference in numerous lives. You have chosen a noble cause, one that can make a tremendous impact on many.

In researching the responsibilities of these leaders, many questions came to mind. Unless it is a brand-new institution, and you are the first in the doors, someone tread the path before you. What groundwork did they lay? What impression did they leave behind? Do you follow that course, or do you begin new groundwork for a different path? When do you implement changes? How do you handle a conflict with an irate parent, teacher, or student? How do you handle an explosive situation, such as an alleged molestation case between a student and a teacher? How will you prepare teachers for new curriculum? How will you discipline your students? Who will be your mentor?

The questions are endless, the answers: priceless.

In Your First Year as a Principal: Everything You Need to Know That They Don't Teach You in School, you will find answers for these questions and more. You will hear from veteran principals and tap into their wisdom; entry-year principals who have just recently lived what you are now experiencing will share their stories, too. Principals, like teachers, are taught steps to handle certain situations, but the truth is, their game plans do not always work. No one knows what he or she will do in any given situation until they are standing in the thick of it. To facilitate the handling of any situation, this book will provide you with suggestions, advice, jokes, sad stories, happy endings, and insights into what you might expect.

This is by no means a step-by-step guide to tell you how to handle your job. All incidents vary, and one must take action — or not — accordingly. This book is merely a reference tool for ideas and direction. It is designed to let you know that you are not alone. In addition, it is meant as a testimony to remind you not only that what you are doing is a work of significant magnitude, but also to reassure you that there are people cheering for you and thanking you for prioritizing the education of their children. It is because of leaders such as yourself that many children grow up to be contributing members of society, confident adults, and upstanding examples for their own children.

For those of you who strive to make our schools positive learning environments for our children, I would like to say with sincere gratitude, thank you.

CASE STUDY: WORD FROM THE EXPERTS

Preliminary Advice for First-Year Principals

- "New principals tend to think they must have all the answers all of the time. The best advice given to me at the start of my administrative career was that very few decisions need to be made immediately. I have lived by that, and it has served me well."
  — **Nancy Graham**

- "It is important to pick your battles. I always use the measuring stick of 'is it good for kids' to help me decide what to fight about and what to let go. There will always be one more silly thing that somebody thinks is important, but does it really help kids in a significant way? I feel it is far more important to concentrate on people and building relationships than what program is best for this or that. Kids and parents, and even most teachers, pretty much do not really care what reading or math program you are using, but they all care very much about your relationship with them."
  — **John Fielding**

- "It is better to take your time before reacting to a situation. It will give you a different perspective if you take the time to get all the facts before making a hasty decision." — **John Redd**

- **Tret Witherspoon** thinks the most important factors are having "great time management and delegating responsibilities to others on the leadership team. It is impossible for one person to complete all the required assignments. In addition, it provides an opportunity for others to utilize their leadership abilities. I also synchronize my smartphone with my calendar on Outlook® to keep up with appointments and other important assignments. Prioritize responsibilities. Search out teachers who have an interest in leadership, and put them to work."

- When discussing the burdensome responsibilities on principals, Tammy Brown suggests handling them "one at a time. I try to do the paperwork and office tasks early in the morning or after dismissal so that I can be in classrooms, halls, and cafeteria interacting with teachers and students as much as possible. Something often comes up that must be dealt with immediately, but most often, things can be prioritized. Try not to do everything in your in-box every day. It is OK to leave something for the next day."
  — Tammy Brown

- "Sit back and watch. If the teachers loved the previous principal, why can it not work for you? I remember hearing the secretary say, 'I do not know if I can work for him. He's a baby.' I just watched and took notes, talked with the teachers, and waited until we were halfway through the year before I even talked about change."
  — Oliver Phipps

- **Robert Spano** cautions to beware of "trying to do too much yourself. Be a good listener to your staff. Do not make decisions in isolation. Form committees or small groups of staff [for] discussion prior to making decisions."

CHAPTER 1

Assessing the Situation

While in college, you were introduced to a long list of duties you needed to learn in order to become a principal. This list included everything from directing maintenance for the school building to implementing a new curriculum. What the list did not detail was how complicated and trying it can be to succeed in this most important profession, or how overwhelming the job truly is, especially at the beginning.

School has not yet started, so this is a good time to get a feel for your new "home away from home." Walk the halls and stroll the school grounds; look around the classrooms, the gymnasium, the lunchroom, the custodian's room, the boiler room, and every other nook and cranny. Observe the characteristics of this building, and listen to what it tells you. Thousands of young lives will pass through these halls, and you will have an effect on every one of them. Study the school's layout, and know it by heart before the year begins. Learn the school's history, the culture of the area, and the community. Familiarize yourself with the ideas, expectations, and dreams that the community holds for its children's education, as well as their past disappointments and complaints.

In order to succeed as a good leader, you must assess the educational institution in which you are now in charge, and then create a strategy that will help you succeed in achieving your goals. You have the job; now it is up to you to wear all the assorted hats you will find waiting for you in the closet of your office. The first step to making your school all it can be is up to you alone, but it is one of the easier steps of the millions you will take throughout your career.

Begin by assessing your situation with a glance at some of the procedural duties you are expected to implement. Take notes on which areas you will need to study in your own institution; decide where your weak areas lie, and think about how you can improve them or learn from them. Here are some tactical tasks for you to consider:

- Implement educational programs and curriculum development.
- Put into operation developmental curriculum for students.
- Observe teaching in the classroom and apply instructional strategies.
- Understand the legislature and laws of your state, district, and community.
- Mandate and disperse monies where needed.
- Establish public relations with the community.
- Coordinate an auxiliary support system or maintain the ones in place.

- Hire, fire, retain, and promote personnel.
- Provide resources and training for your educators.
- Coordinate school activities.
- Assess student accomplishments, and implement strategies to continually improve student achievements.
- Create a safe school environment.
- Set high standards for student learning.
- Be responsible and self-reliant.
- Continue to pursue high levels of learning.
- Maintain discipline standards.

Although this list may not seem too overwhelming at first glance, as a whole it is a large undertaking. It is also merely a fraction of what a good leader needs to do in order to define his or her position and achieve goals set after an assessment.

CASE STUDY: WORD FROM THE EXPERTS

How Former First-Year Principals Assessed Their New Institutions and Chose Curricula

- "Our district has a data warehouse that has updated demographics, test results, and school improvement plans available to view. Those were used as a starting point. Teachers assess students frequently and report their progress through class data sheets. We meet to discuss the information on those sheets, to determine if the district curriculum and materials are successful or if intervention strategies are needed. Our district has committees to select curriculum materials from a state-approved list. We use research-based intervention materials as well." — **Tammy Brown**

- "The curriculum in our district is used by all the schools. Each school has a representative on the committee. For example, this year we are in process of choosing a reading series. Every school had the opportunity to have a member on the committee. Each school representative brought back the top three choices to their schools, and the faculty voted on their top choice. We also use our Title I funds to host an after-school tutoring program for our lowest quartile of students. That curriculum is chosen by the teachers."
— **Katherine Munn**

- "I accessed the institution by evaluating past years' data, including attendance. I also interviewed current teachers to find their opinion of school climate, curriculum, discipline, scheduling, parent involvement, et cetera. Many of the curriculum and instructional ideas came from ideas from my previous school, where I served as assistant principal. I also received input from our Regional Educational Service Agency (RESA) and from the Georgia State Leadership Facilitator." — **Tret Witherspoon**

When you are hired to be a principal, the normal steps are to begin planning for the school year immediately. You may be lucky and find that the previous principal did some of the planning for you, but even if this is the case, you must be sure to review these plans and create your own vision of what needs to be done. If you are hired in the middle of the school year, you will find that things will move along without much, if any, of your input, but you should observe everything possible and take notes for the following year.

During the months before school begins, you can look over student achievement records, review the local assessments that are used to report student progress, and meet your staff. After school resumes, be sure to revisit the staff in-house. Assessing student records and achievements will give you an idea of where the curriculum— or the teaching staff — is succeeding or failing. If there are weak areas, observe the class, and study the teaching methods and tools that are used. This will come later, however; for now, you must learn all you can on your own. Summer is also a good time to assess the buildings and schedule any modifications necessary. When these mentioned tasks are done, or at least under way, it is time to look at the budget and examine where funds have been spent in the past.

Once teachers and staff return to school for the coming year, you will need a checklist of people to speak with. This register should have the name of every teacher, coach, counselor, custodian, secretary, food service worker, media member, and parent involved with your school. This is where the assessment of the inner workings of your educational institution will begin. It is also the beginning of establishing relationships with your personnel. When school resumes, you will want to walk the halls again — watching, observing, learning, introducing yourself, and getting to know the ins and outs of students and teachers, your style of supervision, and the atmosphere surrounding you. This activity has a simple goal — to make you visible. It is the best way to establish yourself as the authority figure, but more important, it is the best way to reassure your students and staff that you are accessible.

There are other, less procedural duties that you are expected to perform, as well as the tactical tasks. These responsibilities tend to rest along the lines of developing and maintaining relationships with the community, personnel, and students of your institution. These undertakings may not rate at the top of the list in significance for some administrators, but principals should take note that, without addressing these points, you have a lesser chance of being successful elsewhere. The following list details the necessary elements every principal should strive to attend to:

- Establish good relationships with all students and teachers.
- Attain excellent standing with parents and community.
- Help set up and maintain a parent/teacher committee.
- Attend after-school functions.
- Provide time for students, teachers, and parents.
- Lead and support for your teachers.
- Supply resources, such as lesson planners or district calendars, to your personnel.
- Show interest in your students' needs and accomplishments.
- Promptly reply to letters, e-mails, and phone calls.
- Support librarians, coaches, counselors, and other personnel by asking about their needs.
- Meet with representatives of local community education partners.
- Be involved with students' emotional welfare.
- Be visible to students and staff.
- Recognize and reward teacher achievement.
- Be supportive of school culture — the beliefs, organizations, and behaviors that characterize the school.
- Attend ceremonies, and affirm student achievement.
- Be a role model.

The two lists previously reviewed are by no means an exaggeration. If anything, they are short when compared to the living, breathing list of duties a principal must face. However, be assured you can achieve these tasks and many more. Many great leaders have walked the halls before you and succeeded; you, too, can become the kind of principal that will leave an impact on those you guide.

A Principal's Priorities

"If students, staff, and parents feel safe at our school, then everything else should fall into place."

Barry Pichard, principal
Sunrise Elementary School
Palm Bay, Florida

When you were hired for this position, the superintendent and school board informed you where your school was lacking and explained what they want accomplished, or they informed you of its success and said it was up to you to keep the attainment intact. What they did not tell you was how to accomplish either goal, whether it be achieving success or maintaining it.

Now that the job is yours, the weight of countless responsibilities sits on your shoulders, and you may feel slightly intimidated, possibly even afraid. Although it is natural to feel that way, keep in mind that you were chosen for this position for a reason: because your superiors have faith in your abilities and know your priorities are in order.

CASE STUDY: WORD FROM THE EXPERTS

Their Top Priorities as Principals

- "Staffing — make sure it is complete with people who share your vision. Budget — make sure all monies are accounted for. Inventory — all is accounted for. Most important, make sure all the children are learning." — **Oliver Phipps**

- "I would like to leave a legacy of pride. I want students, parents, teachers, and community to see Central as an academic and aesthetic asset." — **Pamela C. Mitchell**

- "Relationships between staff and students; between staff and staff; between staff and parents, et cetera. Relationships matter. When they are in line, the other stuff all works out so much more smoothly." — **Nancy Graham**

- **Barry Pichard** said the most important thing to him is the "safety of students, all staff, and parents. If students, staff, and parents feel safe at our school, then everything else should fall into place. Good learning, good teaching, satisfaction from the parents that their students are happy with our school and their progress in the academics."

- "Support your staff. Create an environment that is safe and conducive to learning. Be able to listen and make good decisions based on what is best for your students." — **Robert Spano**

- "Give teachers the support, materials, equipment, and confidence to do their jobs so that they can increase student achievement. Encourage parents to become involved in their child's education. Create a climate where teachers and administrators are on the same page and communicate with each staff member effectively. Do not loose sight of the ball: student achievement." — **Leonard Weiss**

• "My top priorities as a principal are to provide the best academic education I can for all my students, keep them physically and emotionally safe, and make them feel happy to come to my school." — **James Gasparino**

• "I want to make sure that none of my students leave without a diploma and the absolutely essential skills and knowledge he or she will need in either college or a career." — **Chet Sanders**

• "My top priority is to make sure we have a safe and comfortable place to learn and grow." — **John Redd**

During the interview process for this book, it did not take long to realize there were many similar answers among participating principals. The question, "What are your top personal priorities as a principal?" received the same answer from each of them: the "safety of students." It is obviously a main concern of many principals in the school system today.

This is truly a tremendous responsibility you, as a principal, will carry in your years as an educational leader. Parents think it is sometimes hard to be responsible for one, two, or three kids. How about 200, 300, or even as many as 500 students? This is a weight you will be consistently aware of, but few parents think of, until the unimaginable happens.

When veteran principals verify that "safety" is their top priority, first-year principals should take note. The possible threat of violence erupting in your school is a concern you must learn to deal with. When asked about the possibility of violence in schools, all new and veteran principals agreed it is a concern for which they and the school boards have thoroughly prepared.

Parenting and education are the two most important factors in determining a child's future, and the principal's job is second only to a parent's. This fact should weigh heavily on a principal's shoulders, especially a first-year principal. Unfortunately, there is much more at stake than the mere future of an infinite number of students — your responsibility extends beyond the doors of your establishment. Once your students leave your hallowed halls, much of the result of their adulthood rests on you. Who they become as learners, educators, and members of society is a part of your responsibility as well as their parents'. If they become contributing members of society, it can have an effect on your school's community, your state, your country, and in a way, the whole world.

But do not panic. The fact that you took this job indicates you have a sincere interest in education and the welfare of your students. This fact alone is the foundation on which your leadership will bud, bloom, grow, flower, and flourish. Because of your passion, you will touch many souls and leave an everlasting impression. It is up to you whether that impression is good or bad.

The question now is: What are your priorities? The job is yours, but what are you going to do with this institution? Recall the two lists from earlier — you are familiar with the tactical tasks and the necessary elements for which you are responsible. There are certain tasks you must do because they are in the best interest of the students and because they are in the fine print of your contract. Other tasks, however, should be accomplished to achieve success in the areas spelled out in your job description. It is the way to a much smoother road, as well as a happier student body, staff, and principal.

Your first priority must be your students and personnel. You may wonder, why the teachers? Their jobs may seem to be clear-cut, but in order to assess the situation in your educational institution, you must have your teachers' help. They are invaluable resources and perform the following tasks:

- Teach students and help them achieve academic success
- Become a source of information on how the students are performing
- Be a source of information regarding the students' emotional welfare and safety
- Give information as to where old curricula are failing and ideas as to what kind of new curricula are needed
- Help assess and implement new ideas, strategies, and curricula
- Help with time-consuming tasks of leading organizations, forming committees, attending meetings, and public relations
- Help boost morale of students and other staff members

This list demonstrates how important it is to establish good relations with your teachers. Without their support, your job will be impossible to perform. The best way to support your teachers is to let them know you respect their positions. Prove to them that you will be there when they need you, and take their input seriously. To assure your teachers, try the following:

- Talk to them one-on-one and let them know you value their positions and opinions.
- Ask for their ideas, thoughts, and personal opinions on anything they feel needs to be noticed, rectified, or changed.
- Let them know your door is always open.
- Communicate that they are invaluable, and that you need their help and support.
- Take notes, and follow up with them, even if it means disappointing them with bad news.
- Consider writing up a questionnaire seeking their suggestions for future reference.
- Ask for a list of needs for their classrooms.
- Assure them you will do everything possible to make their job easier.

While you have been reading about the importance of your teachers and students, you may have forgotten something else that is extremely important — where would the teachers and students be without you?

In assessing your situation, you have now realized your first resource for success is you. Yes, you. You are the leader of the institution. You are the one invaluable resource your teachers need to produce successful students. Without you, their job is impossible. Without you, the students cannot succeed and move to the next level of their lives.

The second realization is that, in order for you to succeed as a leader, you need a good working relationship with your teachers and successful students. A successful educational relationship is no different from the hallways you will now walk — traffic flows two ways. To begin your school year on a positive note, ideas and support must also flow both ways.

You are assessing and learning about your school. Your teachers can give you more information than necessary, but be warned — it is still the beginning of the year. Do not barge into the school with a list of changes that stretches across the football field. Do not demand drastic changes be implemented within the first week. This kind of action causes poor attitudes and distrust, and it will cause you to look like a greenhorn or a dictator.

Another word of caution: Be careful about making promises. If you make promises you cannot keep, you will cause major damage to what could be resourceful relationships. Always take all requests seriously and give each of them careful consideration, but never promise a result, immediate or otherwise. Even if you must refuse a request, follow up with a discussion and explanation. Diplomacy means everything in your position.

With reviewing student success and failure from the previous year and taking notes of your teachers' input on the subjects you need to know and understand thoroughly, you now have assessed a large and important part of your situation. Although this is just another small step in achieving success, you should feel good in knowing it is an imperative measure that will create a much smoother path, not only this year, but for the coming year as well.

CASE STUDY: WORD FROM THE EXPERTS
Common Mistakes to Avoid

- "Perhaps the most common mistakes made by first-year principals involve decision making. Principals have to make decisions all the time. Some are managerial in nature, some of far-reaching consequences. First-year principals need to recognize that not all decisions need to be made immediately. It is necessary to be able to differentiate what needs to be settled right away and what situations require reflection and input from others. First-year principals may want to do everything right away, and by themselves. It is difficult, if not impossible, to get buy-in from others if they did not have a voice in the decision-making process." — **James Gasparino**

- "Beginning principals almost always fall into the trap of feeling like they need to be everything to everybody. It is important to understand that you cannot do that — either physically, academically, or emotionally. If you are too tired to move, you are no good to anybody else. You do not really have to know and do everything yourself. That said, you do need to know those things that do require your attention and those that you can let others handle. Granted, this is a lot easier to say once you have some experience, but the advice is still to try to get to that point as soon as you can." — **John Fielding**

- **Jory Westberry** advised avoiding "thinking you should have all the answers" or "thinking you should be able to make all decisions quickly."

- **Pamela Mitchell** said it is a common mistake to forget "that there are 24 hours in a day. You will never catch up! Set a time to end your day, go home, and relax. If you take your work home, make it something that you need to do for tomorrow — you will feel like you accomplished something." Mitchell also advises that first-year principals not make the mistake of thinking that "change is easy. Open your eyes more than your mouth."

- **Barry Pichard** said many principals make the mistake of "forgetting how it is to walk in a teacher's shoes. Principals — not only first-year, but as we mature — need to remember how it is in the classroom. It is one of the toughest jobs around." Teachers must deal with "many demands from administrators, parents, and the students themselves."

- **Barbara Belanger** said a common mistake for first-year principals is "feeling like you can do everything yourself. You can avoid this by finding out whom you can delegate to, but [make sure it is someone] who can still keep you informed and updated on what you need to know. Also, find other principals who you can call on to help you find answers to those unknown questions you meet up with."

- "The number one mistake is to go into a school and not learn both the culture and the 'hidden' culture of the building. It is important to just sit back, listen, and learn. I think it is also good to earn and give respect." — **Roy Miller**

- "Many first-years want to make too many changes too quickly. Some also feel they have to do everything by themselves. The biggest [mistake] is to come on too strong and feel they have to show who is boss. If you have to ever remind them who the boss is, you have a problem." — **Michael Miller**

Following in the Previous Principal's Footsteps

One important factor your professors might have overlooked is the previous principal that you will have to follow. This factor may cause you much joy and relief, or it may create untold problems in your new job. It is wise to consider these two scenarios and contemplate ways to deal with each one, because like it or not, one of these two possibilities applies to your current situation.

If you are fortunate, the previous leader of your school left you in a good position. If this is the case, you might, at first, consider yourself lucky. You may soon come to realize, however, that this is not necessarily the case. A great leader leaves big shoes to fill, and it is possible that your teachers, staff, students, administrators, and even the community may see you lacking in leadership skills before you even get started. The community and populace of your school will be assessing you from the beginning.

Before taking over the previous principal's chair, you felt relieved to be following an exceptional leader. After all, he left an establishment that was running smoothly and was considered a success. Then the day came when you entered that office, took a seat in that revered chair, and realized something unexpected. You can admit it: You are new and inexperienced, and you are scared to death that you will not be able to fill his or her shoes. Rest easy. It is all right that you feel intimidated, and it is perfectly understandable. Before you decide you might have made a mistake in taking the job, take comfort in knowing that all first-year principals feel the same at the beginning of their career — regardless of whom they follow. The best advice one can give a new principal in this situation is to remember the students and staff are experiencing this transition, too. Be patient, show that you respect their feelings, and understand that respect only comes with time.

"Make a friend with another administrator and be able to share experiences."

John Redd, principal
Bellevue Junior High
Bellevue, Ohio

The overwhelming tasks you are required to perform on a daily basis are almost limitless. You are responsible for everything from instructional leadership to managing day-to-day activities. Your school's previous principal might be a good mentor, one who can give advice and feedback. With today's schools facing a reduction in budgets, diminishing resources, and constant social changes, you will want to use all the resources available. A good mentor provides a priceless supply of information, feedback, moral support, and understanding. You will want to have someone accessible to provide you with this comfort. Most states are implementing mentoring programs for teachers and principals. Hawaii and the Pacific Region have institutions principals can call for consultation. Ohio has redesigned a new program for entry-year principals that includes two unique elements: an induction program for first-year-principals and a mentoring component for principals and assistant principals. In Ohio, there are two associations principals can turn to for help in their efforts to improve education: the Ohio Association of Elementary School Administrators (OAESA) and the Ohio Association of Secondary School Administrators (OASSA). All states offer some type of an association to help improve education and the quality of school leadership.

The following details the OAESA's stated mission:

- To bring about a more complete understanding of the objectives of the elementary and middle-school administrators

- To work for the continuous improvement of Ohio's elementary and middle-level schools

- To cooperate with organizations that share mutual interest in promoting the cause of quality education.

The OASSA's mission is "to provide high standards of leadership through professional development, political astuteness, legislative influence, positive public relations, and collaboration with related organizations."

As you can see from these few examples, good leadership for our children's education is imperative. The job of leading in an educational environment is stressful; therefore, guidance, advice, and feedback are just some of the qualities a mentor can provide. Another priceless resource a mentor can bring to the table is being able to understand your position and your responsibilities. A mentor is a confidante, a good listener, and can help alleviate stress.

Following an ineffective principal can be cause for major hurdles and headaches. Because of bad leadership, you may experience trust issues from staff, students, and the community. The curriculum will most likely be outdated, tools for teaching may be practically nonexistent, and the building may be falling down around you. In order to repair the damage left by the previous principal, you must first understand it will take time. On your entry as the new principal, you may experience reactions as severe as hostility.

Another possible scenario is facing resentment from staff members who were contenders for the job you now hold. You may be able to win some over by adding them to your various teams, acknowledging their talents, and using their abilities for the betterment of your school. Others, however, may never be won over, and you may have to accept this fact.

If you are following a bad leader, your first approach may be to tap into your resources. Budgets may be limited, but teachers can and do teach effectively without state-of-the-art equipment. The solution is not the software or technology, but the people. Your people will deliver solutions and ideas on how to work around the budget to make your institution a success. Good teachers want students to receive a good education. If they know their leader wants the same, they will be more than happy to help you achieve this goal.

A good leader should, of course, have the ability to lead. It is not necessary for you to take on all the responsibility alone. However, it is imperative that you allow your personnel to know that you not only need help, but also you welcome it, too. Many times, a new principal may take a job without knowing the principal who left. He or she may have refused to help others or to allow others help him or her.

You may feel somewhat isolated and lonely at the beginning, but there are things you can do to improve the relationships you wish to have with your staff and students. Remember, it is important as a leader to be seen. You will not receive help or respect if you hide in your office, sitting behind your desk, waiting for the end of the day. You must be seen by students and staff in order to define who you are and why you are there.

A school haunted by the lingering shadow of an ineffective leader may take more time to get organized. On the other hand, once your personnel and students realize your good intentions, you will most likely find them sincere in their gratitude.

You are taking a position that will seem, at the least, overwhelming, and at most, impossible. A good mentor can relieve your certainty that this job is a lost cause, and he or she can help you maintain a much-needed positive attitude. Imagine making a list of the qualities of principals you have known. The list should include, at the very least: honest, fair, dependable, trustworthy, organized, calm, consistent, supportive, and energetic.

CASE STUDY: WORD FROM THE EXPERTS

The Importance of Mentors

- **Tammy Brown** said she has mentors "both formally and informally. One is a director in the district office, and one is a principal. They both have several years of principal experience. When faced with a difficult, but obvious decision, and I wanted to be sure I was doing the right thing, my mentor told me the best way to handle the situation was head-on. If I felt strongly about my decision, it was not going to help to wait and communicate my decision, but to just do it."

- "I do not have a mentor, but could desperately use one. My school is the only school in the district." — **Tret Witherspoon**

- **Barbara Belanger** said her mentor "was the principal in a school where I was a teacher. She saw leadership abilities in me and involved me in many experiences to widen my view of her position. She encouraged me to go to graduate school and to meet the requirements of an administrator. I was later appointed her assistant principal at the school. She taught me how to hire the best and the brightest of teachers, which I feel is my strongest asset."

- "Bob Donaldson — former area superintendent — knew my pain and worked with me for hours on end until I figured it out myself. He would always say, 'Now, you came up with that idea yourself, and I think that it is pretty good.'" — **Pamela C. Mitchell**

- "My principal and my mentor had opposite leadership styles. This allowed me to see where my style was." — **Michael Miller**

- "I have a fabulous mentor. When I was being moved at the direction of the superintendent from a brand new school I had opened just a year before to a school where all administrators were being removed and a team of us were going in to fix a mess, they called us the 'dream team,' as if that would make us any happier about the move; my mentor called and asked if I was crying. I said, 'Of course, I am.' Her response: 'Then get in the bathroom until you are finished. No one needs to see you cry. They need to see your strength and understanding that you work for an organization.' That was the end of my public tears … to this day." — **Nancy Graham**

- "I had two great mentors. Diane Okoniewski was my principal when I was an assistant principal. I was with her for six-and-a-half years. She and I had a great relationship. We actually used to walk when we had meetings in the evenings just to get out of the building. We would start walking down the street, and parents, neighbors, and students would come out and talk to us.

Sometimes the students would be on their bikes riding along side of us. [We] had a great time. Joseph O'Brien provided me [with] a lot of opportunities when I was teaching for him to have some administrative duties or experiences. The experiences that he provided prepared me for my AP position. He was a great cheerleader for me and my professional career." — **Barry Pichard**

• **Leonard Weiss** said his mentor gave him "very good advice and always told me, 'There is no need to be heavy-handed when dealing with people. Everyone knows you are in charge.'"

Using Your Staff

If you look back at the lists of tactical tasks and necessary elements of procedural duties you must oversee, you will notice the value of good teachers. In implementing educational programs and curriculum development, there is no one who can better inform you of what is needed in each classroom. Teachers are the ones who put into operation the developmental curricula for your students. When you observe classes and suggest instructional strategies, your teachers apply those strategies. The educators inform you of the classroom needs, just as your librarian informs you of library needs. All this information will help you decide the best way to disperse the budget. Staff can also help you foster public relations with the community, take coordinating roles in auxiliary support systems and school activities, and ease some of the weight that rests on your shoulders. Your personnel can keep you up to date on student achievement and student welfare.

Without the support and helping hands of your teachers and staff, you will have a hard time establishing good relationships with your students and their parents. Having a teacher volunteer to serve as a representative for the school's administration during parent-teacher committee meetings is an important resource. With all your responsibilities, you will be stretched thin, so it is good to have a few teachers attend school functions when you cannot.

Your staff can also provide time for your students and parents to come to them with any issues or concerns. In doing so, they can also keep you informed of any needs, accomplishments, conflicts, and/or emotional concerns.

If you know your staff is capable of handling pressing issues, you will be comfortable focusing your attention elsewhere. If you have a high-quality food service leader, you will know that the menu is in good hands, so you can concentrate on more important matters. A first-rate counselor is going to tell you if there is a problem you should be aware of. Good coaches will take care of sports needs and players so that you do not have to look over their shoulders. Mrs. Smith, the fantastic English teacher you inherited, will attend all the PTO/PTA meetings, allowing you much-needed time to review those new test categories the state is implementing next year. The custodian will be more than happy to do a good job for you and your students for no reason other than the respect he or she is given. You secretaries will be friendly because you recognize their hard work. Bus drivers will like you because you take the time to talk to them and inquire if all is running smoothly.

Never forget that parents, volunteers, and student teachers are important. If you take the time to speak with them and show respect, they will be supportive and helpful.

Quality personnel are imperative, and they are a fine resource for a good principal. Great leaders are not afraid to let others lead. Brilliant leaders search for others to lead. Using your staff in this way is not only beneficial for your time management, but also for your peace of mind. One thing you must be aware of in using your staff for leading roles is that you must never assume all is going smoothly. You must take the time to meet with your chosen leaders, review the information available about the decisions being considered, and sit in on some meetings occasionally to stay on top of situations.

By using your staff appropriately, you will have more time to devote to other, more pressing matters. After all, you are needed for things as simple as standing in the hallways during class change to discovering resources and tools for your teachers. As you can see, your staff is invaluable in helping lighten the load of your unyielding responsibilities. It is in your personal interest, as well as that of your educational institution, to create a good relationship with your staff and use them where needed.

A Clear View

These are only some of the places you must look in order to assess your institution. There are so many responsibilities that one must make a list of priorities and stick to that list to avoid burning out before the year even begins. So far, you have studied past student achievements to get an idea of where curricula and/or teachers may be succeeding or failing. You have plans to sit in during classroom time to get an overview of your teachers' abilities, their disciplinary actions, and their use of the curriculum to decide what, if anything, needs to change. You have a list of all personnel so that you may talk with each of them one-on-one to determine what their needs are and discover the strongest candidates for future committee leaders. You know that the best way to overcome a lingering shadow left by a previous leader is to gain the respect of your staff and students, and in turn, to give them the respect they deserve. You know the importance of a good mentor and have begun looking for one or have found one. You have an idea of good resources for tools and training for teachers, and you plan to deal with these issues as soon as you have their list of needs. You have verified the tactical tasks you must accomplish, but more important, you have identified the necessary elements you will need to implement in order to succeed in those tasks. The overall view is becoming clear, and once the year has begun, you will be better prepared to fill the gaps that exist on the path from point A to point B.

CASE STUDY: WORD FROM THE EXPERTS

Things They Wish They Had Known Before Starting the Principalship

- "I would have liked to have learned more on how to involve community stakeholders in the decision-making process, evaluating teachers and staff, managing extracurricular activities such as athletic events, and creating a disaster prevention management plan." — **Tret Witherspoon**

- "One: how to interview personnel more effectively in positions such as custodians and cafeteria staff. I think principals are pretty good at interviewing instructional personal as well as office staff, but cafeteria and custodial positions are usually ones we have never held. Two: how to work with the local media in a crisis situation. Our district has done a good job of preparing principals once you are hired, but this is a position that many of us have not yet experienced until the media shows up on campus." — **Barbara Belanger**

- "No matter what you plan and how you plan it, your schedule is at the mercy of things that you cannot control — do not think that you are incompetent because you do not get to the bottom of your list. Students care about you, but they also are afraid of the authority they see in the position. If you want to get the pulse on your school, gain their trust. Spend more time talking with your students than you do in your office. Principals need to remember that teachers need constant affirmation that they are valuable." — **Pamela C. Mitchell**

- "My biggest initial 'aha' as an administrator was that if I say it, then it matters or must be true to those who hear it. The opportunity to just participate in a conversation with staff members disappeared as soon as I got my title." — **Nancy Graham**

- **Robert Spano** said he wished someone had warned him to "be sure you are able to handle people second-guessing your decisions and be prepared to spend easily 50 to 60 hours a week on the job."

- "I would have liked to have known how much attention I would receive and being the topic of conversation I would become. Also, I would have liked to have known that I did not have to do everything myself. In fact, my authority was enhanced when I realized that I should share it. Always remember that, essentially, we are in a people business. Also, I wish I knew when somebody screwed up, it became my problem and screw-up." — **James Gasparino**

- "I would have benefited from having been exposed to some of the comprehensive reform efforts, such as [Ted] Sizer's work with the Coalition of Essential Schools. Having examples of best practices that are producing positive results with students helps principals build a vision for the kind of school they would like to aim toward." — **Chet Sanders**

CHAPTER 2
The Gap Analysis

Now that school has begun, you have likely begun to assess the situation, including how far it is from point A, where you educational institution is to point B, and where your educational institution should be. Some of you may feel even more overwhelmed than you did when you first sat behind your new desk. The solutions will vary for each of you; there is no set answer. Although this may be comforting to some, it may be disconcerting for others.

In determining where you are and where you want to be, you need a course of action. First, you need a course.

Investigating the reasons why your school is not where it should be can result in some disquieting answers. When the students are failing or falling behind in their studies, the teachers are failing the students. If the teachers are failing, the principal is failing as a leader. The question then becomes, why? In order to establish the "why," a principal accepts the responsibility of examining the curriculum, sits in during class time to evaluate teaching methods, and studies the community to search for better-suited curricula. An outstanding leader will also take the time to learn something about each individual student.

You might find that your institution is having problems because a portion of the student population is Hispanic, with English being their second language. You may have also discovered you have no Spanish-speaking teachers. The solution to this problem is relatively simple: find new curricula to alleviate the language barrier, hire teachers with Spanish-speaking capabilities, and follow this up with a study of the community and its future needs; implement extra curricula that will serve as suitable solutions. But what if your school is made up of English-speaking students in a middle-income neighborhood with low scores on state tests and academia? How do you identify the problem, and how do you implement a solution?

You have reviewed the state test results and discovered that the scores are average or poor. You then checked the students' academic records, but found they are lacking in many areas. It is no surprise that students score low on state standardized tests as well as in the classroom. However, how can students score average on state tests but poorly in the classrooms? It could be the teachers have been teaching for the state tests. According to studies, a common dilemma among some schools with this problem was that they focused their curriculum to facilitate better scores on state tests; this was a knee-jerk reaction to demands for test results to be higher. This is not something a good leader would have his or her teachers do. A study of schools that led the way in standardized testing found that those principals were more focused on what was best for their students, not what would directly result in good test results. These principals took the existing student achievement principles and added what was necessary to help students achieve good test results. The bottom line is that the best leaders maintain perspective and keep their priorities in order.

If scores are low in academia as well as state testing, the first place to look is the classroom. It could be the teachers are not doing their job correctly, are doing it poorly, or have no tools with which to teach. This deduction leads to the dreaded problem of the bad teacher, also referred to as the "bad apple."

There can be numerous reasons for low student achievement, but once you discover what the problems are, you must find solutions. Sometimes the best solution may take time to resolve the issues at hand. Sometimes the problem may be simple, but reaching the proper solution may take more effort. Either way, it is your job as leader to assess, analyze, close the gap, measure the success or failure of the implemented solutions, and inform your superiors of the results. Simply put, it is up to you to correct the problems.

When one thinks in terms of the problem becoming "my problem," it becomes somewhat clearer and easier to correct, even when it calls for doing something undesirable, which brings us back to the bad apple.

If the answer to your institution's problem is a need of teaching tools, you can assess the budget and find resources for your teachers. If your teachers are not teaching correctly, or if they are teaching poorly but show integrity, a desire to improve, and the potential to do so, you can facilitate professional development services. There are numerous seminars and classes designed to help teachers improve their abilities.

However, some teachers may be past the point of helpful classes. When you are barraged with angry phone calls and visits from parents, and when you witness poor teaching firsthand, the only thing left to do is to deal with the problem directly. As a leader, you must keep in mind that a student who has a weak teacher for a year will fall behind his or her peers. A student who has more than one bad teacher may never catch up. If this is not enough to convince you to force your hand as a principal, you might want to consider an alternative: Remove the student, create improvement plans for the teacher, or both. The easiest solution is to place the student in another classroom, if possible. Why not just fire the teacher? *This subject is explored in detail in Chapter 5.*

In assessing the situation, you may have found a discipline problem in your institution. The discipline of students is mainly up to the teachers, as they are the ones who manage the classrooms. The last resort is to send the misbehaving student to the principal. However, the best way to handle discipline problems is to remedy the problem before the student ends up in the principal's office. Discipline can be a touchy subject, and sometimes it is difficult to find a set rule to use for a solution. Some schools insist on using assertive discipline. Although this may work for some teachers, it does not necessarily work for others. More often than not, though, it is not the rule of discipline being used that poses the problem — it is the teacher.

Mrs. Beresta, a wonderful sixth-grade teacher in Ohio, is a natural when it comes to disciplining her students. If she has a student who insists on acting out, she will approach the student and quietly speak with him or her about the behavior. If need be, she will sometimes take the student into the hallway to have a private conversation about issues bothering the student. Seldom does a student have to be sent to the principal's office. In the same school, there was a fourth-grade teacher who was quite the opposite, however. Mr. Waltin would scream at a misbehaving student, and even went so far as to manhandle a few. The last straw was when he pushed one young man against the wall. The problem in this case was not the form of discipline chosen by the school board, but the teacher's personal choice in how to handle student discipline. Mrs. Beresta's solution was to know her students individually and handle them accordingly. Most students behaved well in Mrs. Beresta's class, most likely due to mutual respect between teacher and students.

When observing a classroom, it is better to enter unannounced. This is the only way you will see the true interaction between teacher and students. The chance to observe with no warning will be short-lived, so you must discern the potential problems and solutions within your first few seconds in room. You also need to log everything that occurs during your sit-in for reference when evaluations take place. *Discipline and dealing with conflict will be discussed in more detail in Chapter 5.*

Curricula and teaching tools are imperative in navigating the best course to take to arrive at point B. In some states, administrators in school district offices oversee curricula and direct subject-area programs. These administrators supervise instructional coordinators and curriculum specialists. In many cases, administrators have transferred primary responsibility for programs to the principals. Principals are now accountable for students meeting national, state, and local academic standards. This adds to your list of responsibilities and is a major problem for principals; most principals must spend the majority of their time attending to management and conflict. Again, your best resource for choosing the best curricula and implementing tools are your teachers. After observing the classrooms, speak with your teachers about what they feel would enhance their teaching skills and students' achievements.

CASE STUDY: WORD FROM THE EXPERTS

Determining the Best Resources for Your Teachers

- "Many times, it comes from the teachers themselves. If they see materials or workshops of interest, and they are in alignment with our school and district goals, we look for funds from our Parent Teacher Organization, grants, or school improvement funds to support teachers." — **Tammy Brown**

- "Curriculum Council (team leaders) and I choose which the best is. Teachers know that when they come to me with a special order that it has to be research-based." — **Katherine Munn**

- "Best resources are always determined by research-proven resources and by talking with other school administrators who have used the resources." — **Tret Witherspoon**

It is easy to discover if one of the institution's problems rests with a bad teacher, but it may be more difficult to determine the issue at hand if this is not the case. One thing you may want to do is learn about each individual student. This is extremely time-consuming, but it is also imperative in determining what is missing at your school. The problems at your school may run deeper than readily apparent at first glance.

There are many students who come from broken or abusive homes, their foundations never solid. The groundwork on which the school's teachers had to expand, therefore, was not what one would consider a good start. If you are running a stable, smooth, educational, encouraging, and safe school, there is a much better chance those students will find their way, especially with the help and guidance of you and your staff. The emotional welfare of your students is in your hands. If you discover that students need emotional support, it is up to you and your personnel to make sure you do all you can to help them.

The following is a list of some of the possible problems your institution may face, as previously discussed:

- Teaching to state standardized tests
- Badly chosen curricula based on community needs
- Possibility of a bad teacher
- School discipline
- Curricula
- Previous leader's shortcomings
- Relations with teachers
- Proper use of staff

Determining the problems is relatively simple. Finding solutions to those problems, however, can be extremely trying and can sometimes seem impossible.

Where to Go From Here

You have evaluated and analyzed your institution, but what is your personal vision for the school? You know what curriculum needs are; what the teachers would like to see in their classrooms; and what the nation, state, and district want in student achievement. The missing link is your personal concept for your institution.

Where your focus lies will demonstrate to your personnel, students, and community what is most important to you; some first-year principals tend to overlook this. If a good relationship with your students and teachers is a top priority, for example, you will not convince anyone of this fact if you spend all your time in your office doing paperwork.

You have assessed the preliminary, checked the structure of the building, talked with your teachers, reviewed student achievements, assessed the curricula, and sought out resources that may be needed in the near future. You are now waiting to sit in on your teachers' class time to evaluate their teaching styles and determine whether they have the necessary tools. You will then take the time to get to know your students individually, not just on paper, and meet the parents at open house or parent-teacher conferences. Talk with your kitchen staff, become acquainted with your custodians, and learn about each extracurricular activity that takes place inside your building. Ascertain who your best teachers are, and determine who your worst teachers might be. Be sure to make an appointment to meet your PTO/PTA president, the media, the academic booster president, the alumni president, the mayor, president of city council, and others involved with the inner workings of your school. Even after you have done all this, however, the job is nowhere near done.

A Contagious Vision

Each principal is a unique individual. Each one has his or her own personal idea of how a school should be run. But do you have an idea of what you want your students to take with them when they receive that diploma and walk out the doors as a student for the last time? Do you know what your vision is?

Vision is the act or power of anticipating that which will or may come to be. It is also described as a vivid, imaginative conception or anticipation.

If you had to guarantee that each of your students would leave your school with one thing, what would it be? To determine exactly what your vision entails, ask yourself these questions: What drives me? What persuaded me to choose this career? When I chose this path, what were my reasons? What did I believe I could do for an educational institution?

It was your passion for giving students good education that brought you to this point in your life. Think back, and recall the thoughts you had when you first decided on this career, because it was those beliefs, those dreams, which brought you to the present. Those thoughts and dreams will guide your plans for your school.

You now know what is expected of you by your administration, the community, and, to some extent, your students. But to truly be successful, you also have to know what you expect of yourself and your staff. Whatever it is, that is your vision.

Once you know what your vision is, what your school's problems are, and what tools and training are needed, you must then outline a strategy to make it happen.

You are the only one who can create your unique, individual vision, but your mentor might be able to help you do so. Being able to talk to someone who knows what you are experiencing and what you mean when you say, "I want my students to feel they are special," is like having a second brain work for you. Your mentor can help you put into words what you feel but cannot say. He or she can help you define your passion, your dream for your institution, and your desire for your students' future.

A principal's vision for his or her school is more than just a dream; it is a possibility. Think about that statement for just a minute. Your vision is not just a dream — it is truly feasible, and you must always remember to follow that dream. Do not give in and decide it is not worth pursuing because it is not tangible. A vision is an anticipation of that which will come; it is something you wish to accomplish, and it is achievable. Just do not forget the most important ingredient in achieving it — your team.

Once you have established your vision, you need to get your teachers on board to in order to achieve it. The easiest way to do so is to be passionate about it. Such profound belief is contagious, especially if you are enthusiastic. Take notice when your staff does something positive; this is a step toward achieving your vision, and whoever takes that step, no matter how small, should be applauded. Praise the custodian for searching through the trash to find a student's retainer. During morning announcements, thank the drama teacher and the students for putting on such a wonderful performance the night before, then go to the classroom, and thank them in person. Applaud the teacher who consistently directs high-achieving students. All these actions on their part are major strides toward making your vision reality. The acknowledgment on your part will encourage further progress.

Another important step toward reaching your ultimate goal is to encourage your teachers and students to experiment. Over the course of the years to come, you will be amazed at how many ideas staff and students share if you take the time to listen and provide them with opportunities to experiment. Regardless of the outcome of any experiment, the attempt should be applauded. Success is wonderful, but failure can be just as important — it is a learning opportunity, cause for innovation. Trying is the key. If your teachers or students are not afraid to try something new, it means they have faith in you.

Listen when Ms. Stephens says, "I think a hands-on approach in Mr. Smith's oceanography class is the way to go." Be enthusiastic that Ms. Stephens made the suggestion, and ask her to help you persuade Mr. Smith to try it. Teachers are hesitant to suggest ideas as they are so often shot down — because of possible liabilities or a lack of funds and/or volunteers, for instance. They begin to wonder, "Why suggest an idea if you know it will be tossed? Why even exert the energy to think of ideas if they will only be belittled?" So when Ms. Stephens looks at you as though you have suddenly sprouted three heads, keep smiling. Keep the enthusiasm bubbling, and again ask for her help in convincing Mr. Smith — remain positive.

Once Ms. Stephens has become infected with your contagious enthusiasm, stay focused on that positive attitude, even in the face of problems or negativity. Say Mr. Smith's first reaction is to share his idea of setting up saltwater and freshwater aquariums for the students to take care of as part of their grades. Everyone is growing excited over the suggestion — until Mr. Smith brings up the lack of funds for this project. Tackle this problem by asking his students for suggestions, and assure him that you will help in every way possible, seeking resources, donations from the community, and volunteers. All of a sudden, what was once an improbable dream is beginning to look possible.

In her book *Gardening in the Minefield: A Survival Guide for School Administrators*, author Laurel Schmidt writes of how she implemented "peer visiting day" to spread her vision. She would teach a class for one period while the assistant principal did the same. This gave two teachers the freedom to observe and ask questions of their peers. She also organized brown bag seminars for lunchtime, giving teachers the opportunity to listen to a guest lecturer while eating lunch.

There are many ways to promote your vision for your school, but it is in your best interest to include the parents. Although this is much easier said than done, it is doable. The key is to remember your students' parents are diverse. You may have supportive parents, involved parents, uninterested parents, and parents who may be waiting for a reason to criticize you. If you take time to include parents by sharing your vision with them and asking for their input, you will win over the majority in due time. You might also gain knowledge, volunteers, resources, and ideas.

Hiring and Firing Teachers

In cards, your hand may only contain one suit, but it will be weak unless you are playing a certain game. The same is true in the educational game — you need quality teachers in all subject areas to be successful.

Bad teachers can be detrimental to your school, and in effect, your career. Getting rid of bad staff is not easy. It can be done, but it comes at a cost. Unfortunately, when school administration tries to fire a bad teacher, it can have a negative effect on district and state funds, teachers' and students' morale, and your sanity. You might not want to take this route if there is an easier way.

To determine if there is a bad teacher on your staff, look for these telltale signs:

- A good teacher will look internally to find the problem if his or her students are doing poorly, while a bad teacher will blame everyone else.

- There is a history of phone calls and angry letters from parents concerning this teacher.

- Students from his or her classes repeatedly come to your office to complain.

- No amount of training or tools improves the situation or teaching technique.

- Students consistently have bad grades.

- Students do well or average in all classes with the exception of this particular teacher.

Once you are certain you have a bad apple on your hands, you must decide what to do with it. Here is where you must choose your battles wisely. Unfortunately, the cost of getting rid of a bad teacher does not outweigh what they hope is only a temporary impact on the students.

In a survey performed by the New Teacher Project in 2007, hundreds of Chicago principals said that 83 percent of poor-performing, tenured teachers are "rarely or never" terminated. A 2002 study in New York found that the average time needed to terminate a teacher was 319 days, while the average cost to complete the termination was $112,000. If the decision was appealed, the cost was almost three times as much. In most states, teachers draw their pay during the dismissal process, which leads to an even higher cost. Most of the time a principal is forced to sign a letter of recommendation, putting the bad teacher in a good position to find another job elsewhere. In this case, you are simply passing the problem to another institution.

Instead of firing bad teachers, most principals attempt to encourage the teacher to improve, grow, and learn to teach better. This is an impossible task for some, but for others, there is usually at least a small amount of improvement. Note that if you do have a bad teacher, you should log everything that is said or done to facilitate progress.

When you evaluate a bad teacher, you may carefully suggest a different approach or method for him or her to try. You could purchase new tools or software, or you might create new curricula. Although these solutions are not guaranteed to make a difference, attempting to help a problem teacher do a better job is in your best interest.

Thankfully, most principals can honestly say the majority of their educators are good teachers. There may be some underperformers, but they can usually be helped to improve their methods. So, how is a principal to overcome deeper teaching issues? The solution is not always in the firing, but in the hiring.

CASE STUDY: WORD FROM THE EXPERTS
Advice on Hiring Teachers

- "Lean on those who have been doing it for some time. A new principal needs to realize that it is OK not to know everything your first few years." — **Roy Miller**

- "Hire people who are enthusiastic about kids and have a willingness to learn." — **Barbara Belanger**

- "Use a committee to do all staff hiring. This way you are getting the buy-in of staff members who will be working with each hire." — **Robert Spano**

- "Do your homework. Check out the applicants' references in great detail. An interview is the worst predictor of job performance." — **Leonard Weiss**

- "Hiring teachers is the most important thing you'll do. Always be sure to call all references and ask probing questions." — **James Gasparino**

- "I believe that hiring teachers — and other staff — is the single most important job that a principal does. It is important to know what you want, what kind of questions will help you sort the applicants into those you want and those you don't, and understand the concept of how they 'fit' with the other teachers and staff at your school." — **John Fielding**

- "More important than knowledge of a subject is the ability to develop healthy relationships with students and fellow teachers." — **Chet Sanders**

- "Look for a little bit of experience, their ability to get along with other people, and have some compassion." — **John Redd**

If you are fortunate enough to have the ability to hire new staff members, do so carefully. Do everything humanly possible to hire exceptional teachers. This will help minimize what few bad teachers you may have; it may even have a positive influence on the bad teachers. To avoid a losing and costly battle, helping your bad teachers and hiring good teachers is usually the best place to focus, instead of allowing the bad apple to become the focal point.

Although interviews do not tell you everything you need to know about a potential teaching candidate, they are helpful in shedding light on each individual's personality, skills, and goals. The following is a list of questions you may want to use when interviewing someone for a teaching position at your school:

- Why did you choose to become a teacher?

- How did your university prepare you to be a teacher?

- What do you feel are your strengths and weaknesses?

- What part of teaching appeals to you most/least?

- What is your philosophy on teaching?

- In your opinion, what is the most important part of teaching?

- How will you incorporate special needs children in your classroom?

- What does diversity mean to you?

- How will you create a positive environment in your classroom?

- How will you integrate technology into your lesson plans?

- Where do you want to be in five years?

- Why do you want to teach in this district?

- What curriculum areas do you feel are your strongest?

- How will you involve parents in the classroom?

- How will you create relationships with your students and their parents?

- What do you think will provide you the greatest pleasure in teaching?

- In what way will you encourage creativity in your classroom?

- Can you describe a successful lesson?

- What do you look for in a principal?

- How would you communicate with administrators?

- What part of this job do you look forward to?

You may also wish to include some behavioral questions. Examples include:

- Describe a time you had to deal with a student who was disrupting your class.

- Describe a team project you have done.

- Tell me about a difficult situation you were in, how you handled the situation, what the outcome was, what you learned from it, and what you would do differently if a similar situation occurred today.

- Describe how you would handle an angry parent who escorts her or his son into the room in the morning, angry that the student was placed in the wrong math or science group.

- Explain what you would say if a parent calls you out of concern for his or her child's low grades.

Use the candidate's responses, as well as his or her qualifications and background, to judge whether he or she is a good fit for the school. It is also important for the teacher to make sure the school is a good fit for him or her, so be prepared to also answer questions about the institution and your vision for it. Hiring a teacher is one of the most important things you will do for your school, so do not take such a decision lightly.

Your Strategy

Your approach will determine whether your institution becomes, or continues to be, successful. It is up to you to be the leader you attended college to become.

As a professor of educational leadership at Indiana State University, Todd Whitaker conducted a study involving 163 middle schools. He found three key differences between effective and less effective principals. One significant difference was that the effective principals viewed all aspects of the school as their responsibilities. If you want to be a superb principal, you must be willing to accept such a large burden. That is the first step in your strategy.

The second step involves your vision. Maintain and feed that vision at every opportunity. Keep a positive attitude, and be sure to applaud those who help make this vision become a reality. If you use your staff wisely, it will benefit you greatly. Your staff is your key to success, just as you are theirs. Your responsibilities are so vast that it is almost impossible to do everything required. Your staff is the place you will find help. They will lighten your load, bring information to your door, help boost morale, serve as a springboard in the community, soothe the ruffled feathers of parents, teach your students well so they will become successful adults, and carry your vision throughout the remaining years of their respective careers.

Your mentor can help you in many ways and is an important asset; he or she will serve as a guide, a helping hand, a sounding board, and a place to find suggestions. A mentor can provide you with peace of mind, which is like gold in your position.

Respect and reflect on the previous leader whose footsteps you follow — this is a key factor in building relationships with your staff. Do not attempt to make them forget someone they held in such high regard. No matter how well organized the previous leader was, make your own lists, and evaluate everything. Be patient, kind, respectful, and understanding. In time, the previous leader will be remembered fondly for the things he or she did. Your position will become defined soon enough.

Keep your priorities in order. Student education is the top priority, but to achieve the best education possible for your students, you must assist your staff in every viable way. If your teachers are educating the best they know how, then improving their skills is the focus. Teach them new and different methods of practice. Provide tools they can use to improve their teaching skills. Allow them time to visit other classrooms and discuss teaching methods with other teachers. Taking care of your teachers is the best way to take care of your students.

Stay out of the office as much as possible. If your focus is on paperwork and phone calls, you will never convince anyone that your top priority is your students' education. Be seen and be heard in order to create productive relationships with your staff.

Praise the good work that takes place in your school every day, and it will be obvious you are a worthy and caring leader.

Treat everyone with respect, and expect the same in return. This cannot be stated enough. Without showing respect, you will never gain respect. This is a two-way street, not only with your staff, but also with the students, their parents, the community as a whole, your administration, your school board, and anyone else who has a hand in education.

CASE STUDY: WORD FROM THE EXPERTS

First-Year Principals on What They Hope to Achieve at Their New Institutions

- "When I began my role as principal, the staff here wanted to feel more connected to one another. I worked hard to set the tone that we would be a team all working together for the success of all students. We have a good feeling here that we are all part of a team, but mostly as grade-level or department teams. I am still working on us being one big team. That was challenging with 30 new teachers to the school this year. Next year we will continue. I will feel successful when we meet that goal, and I hear all staff members talk about the students, not as mine or yours, but as ours." — **Tammy Brown**

- "At this point, [I hope] to maintain an A as the school grade. I feel that I already have most of the faculty and staff on board with me. That is important." — **Katherine Munn**

CHAPTER 3

The Standards

There are set standards all principals are expected to use as guidelines. Several states have adopted these standards, which were set by the Council of Chief State School Officers (CCSSO) and are known as the Interstate School Leaders Licensure Consortium (ISLLC) Standards. These profound words were used to restructure the principal programs at several universities; they were also used as a model to redesign programs for leading principals. The standards state that a principal is a leader who promotes the success of students first and foremost. The wording of the standards leaves no doubt that a principal's top priority is the education, health, and safety of his or her students. The ISLLC Standards can be found — free — in PDF form at **www.ccsso.org/content/ pdfs/isllcstd.pdf**. The booklet may also be purchased for $10 by writing to: Council of Chief State School Officers, Attn: Publications, 1 Massachusetts Avenue NW, Suite 700, Washington, DC 20001-1431.

There are certain untold rules a great principal will follow when dealing with his personnel and students on a daily basis. The first is to show respect for each individual in your building. A quality principal has set standards from which he or she never wavers, integrity being the building block on which these values lie. A good principal will never correct one of his or her teachers in the presence of others. A leader with proper values will not hesitate to applaud his or her teachers or allow them to have the stage when they ask for it. A good leader will listen to every problem that arrives at his or her door with genuine concern and should have a smile for each person he or she passes. An admirable principal will respect each individual he or she deals with, from the custodian to the best teacher in the school. Each student will be given a chance to redeem himself or herself after acting inappropriately, and a compassionate leader will do all he or she can to understand what caused the student to act inappropriately.

As a leader, you must be caring as well as detail-oriented in order to have a well-run environment. You must communicate with the populace of your school. Communication is easier today with e-mail, but communication only through e-mail comes across as cold and impersonal. Face-to-face discussions are appropriate and necessary in order to develop good relationships.

The reality it is that your job as a school leader is complex. Your tasks are innumerable, and at times, they may be overwhelming. Stay focused on learning, teaching, and school improvement —this is how you will succeed.

Honoring the System

By following the ISLLC Standards, you will be able to honor the system. The ISLLC Standards are the moral compass and social principles you must follow for the good of the students and communities you serve. They are designed so that you value, honor, and care for the individuals who comprise your educational community.

Value, honor, and care are strong words that are imperative for school leaders to incorporate into their personal doctrines. Parents put the fates of their children in your hands each day of the week, entrusting you with the care of their most precious possessions. This is the primary reason it is so important for you, as a leader, to honor the system. There is much more at stake than the future of an infinite number of students. Your responsibility spreads from inside the school to beyond the doors of your establishment. Once your students leave your hallowed halls, the adults they become will affect your school's community, your state, your country, and possibly the world as a whole.

You, as principal, are expected to have a hand in shaping your students into contributing members of society; most would not want to carry this burden. The profession you have chosen is noble, but it is up to you to ensure it is carried out in a noble way.

The social fabric of society is changing, with its culture becoming more diverse, poverty increasing, and families becoming more complex;. all of this influences the physical, emotional, mental, and moral welfare of your students, which makes your job as a school leader much more multifaceted than it once was. Everything that happens in the world can, directly or indirectly, affect the students in your care. The economic foundations of our society, the global economy, technological advances, market-based solutions, job losses, diminishing markets, and the ever-changing world of education all have an affect on whether the families in your community are thriving or diminishing. This, in turn, will determine how your students are behaving, or not behaving, in your school. How you handle those students who are being affected by the ever-changing world in which they live will have an impact on their lives, in either a good way or a negative way. The pressure is on you, and in order to be an effective principal, you must live up to the standards.

The ISLLC Standards are the heart and soul of effective leadership. A school community is a living, breathing entity. For quality of life, children must be educated in an exceptional learning environment. Three basic principles form the framework of the ISLLC Standards: knowledge, disposition, and performance. The CCSSO states, "As we became more enmeshed in the work, we discovered that the dispositions often occupied center stage."

A principal's disposition affects the entire working environment of a school. If you are in a foul mood, it will influence everyone around you, everyone those people are around, and so on. Your day-to-day temperament will affect many people, not just one or two. Your school needs you to leave behind whatever problems you might have in your personal life once you reach the school grounds. You have control over your actions, and it is up to you to maintain a good disposition. Your good humor and caring will spread from one person to another, creating an environment that will enhance learning. Like your vision, a good disposition is contagious.

The principal is the center of all action within the school. Everyone goes to the principal with problems involving another person of the school community — teachers, students, staff members, parents, cooks, custodians, PTO/PTA presidents, school board members, the mayor, the media, and even city council members. All things revolve around you, and you are the one who will leave the lasting impression. How you react to a situation; request, devise, and implement a solution; take action; and follow up your actions will determine your relationship with the community and your reputation as a leader. You alone set the tone for the whole school community; make it enthusiastic, genuine, and positive by setting the example.

CASE STUDY: WORD FROM THE EXPERTS

How Well Does College Prepare You for the Job?

- "Just like preparing you to be a teacher, the best learning comes on the job. College helped with the law, finance, and managerial tasks. Since no day is ever the same as the one before, you never know exactly what to prepare for each morning."
— **Tammy Brown**

- "My educational leadership degree taught me many things — financial, curriculum, law — but not how to deal with difficult parents."
— **Katherine Munn**

- "Being a good principal is mostly on-the-job training. For instance, having a parent cursing you out was not in Principal Training 101. Training for the curriculum is there — the paperwork — but the nuts and bolts, you do not get that until you are in this seat."
— **Oliver Phipps**

- "There is no college course nor classroom teaching experience that prepares you for the job as principal. Today's principal must be everything to all people, including parents, community businesspersons and leaders, attorneys, media, et cetera. Oh, yes — did I say teachers and students?" — **Pamela C. Mitchell**

- "I believe each district has a training program that better prepares you for being a principal than college." — **Michael Miller**

- "I am unsure anything can truly prepare one for this job except for time in the chair. I took only one course in personnel, and that was at the doctoral level. Ironically, a large bulk of a principal's time is spent dealing with personnel issues. It is a myth that children create the most challenging times for a principal." — **Nancy Graham**

- "There is no experience better than hands-on [experience]. Book experience is not anywhere near the same as actual school experience." — **Robert Spano**

- "College gives you a theoretical basis for your practice. However, most of what you learn is through experience — in other words, on-the-job training." — **Leonard Weiss**

- "University work, particularly at the advanced degree level, does help prepare us for the principalship in providing the necessary academic and theoretical knowledge needed. However, the necessary experiential knowledge can only be gained through on-the-job training, such as serving as an assistant principal under a good mentor." — **James Gasparino**

- "College coursework provides a good foundation in many areas that the principal deals with. However, much of the knowledge that principals need must be learned over time with experience." — **Chet Sanders**

- "College gives you some basic knowledge, but much of what you need to know, you find out on the job and from your teaching experience." — **John Redd**

What you learned in college will help you set goals, implement curricula and programs, observe classroom teaching methods, understand law and legislature, mandate and disperse monies, coordinate auxiliary support systems, hire and fire, provide resources, prepare your students for standardized tests, and organize school activities and events. These areas are where your skills and knowledge are required. However, there are other areas where skills and knowledge are not enough.

What the colleges and universities cannot prepare you for are the everyday tasks, both small and large. You may deal with disputes, leaking water pipes, broken water fountains, a faulty boiler, a wrecked bus, and a crying student whose parents are in the middle of a bitter divorce. You will handle phone calls and letters of all types. Sometimes there are disasters, adversities, and tragedies, during which you are expected to maintain leadership and remain in control. There will be community events to attend and successes of both staff members and students that will need to be acknowledged and praised. The harmless, but distracting, class clown will become your problem; the food fights your dilemma. You will be required to maintain a good outlook throughout.

In order to deal with everything that comes to your desk, you must maintain a sense of humor when necessary; feel a parent or student's sense of loss, regret, or redemption; control your level of patience; and remember the people you are dealing with might be having a bad day, too. In most situations, it is not necessarily the solution that matters most, but rather how you deal with the problem at hand. You need tact, integrity, and sincerity in order to maintain good relationships within your school community.

Your values and standards as a human being will determine your values and standards as a principal. If you consider your school community your second family, you will produce quality teachers and resourceful students who will then become admirable adults.

A principal must, however, remember that he or she cannot be all things to all people. Trying to please everyone can cause more conflicts than not. It is important to do what you feel is right for the student or the school community as a whole, not just what the person sitting on the other side of your desk wants you to do.

There are some questions you must keep in mind. What is best for the student? What is best for the education of the student? What is best for the school community as a whole? Sometimes the answers may conflict. At that point, you must judge if what is better for the student is necessarily better for the school community as a whole. These decisions are not always easy, but if you are doing the best you can for your second family, they can ask nothing more of you. By being consistent, reliable, and basing your actions on your standards and vision, you will show the school community that you stick to priorities.

A principal must be diplomatic in all situations. You may not say what the person sitting on the other side of your desk wants to hear, but if you say it right, they will most likely leave the office with respect and gratitude. Of course, there will be times when it will not matter what you say or how you say it, but those instances should be few and far between if you always strive to be tactful. If you show genuine concern for the person to whom you are speaking, you will get much further than you would if you simply dismissed others.

During the research process for this book, it became apparent that there is another major change in the educational world — the overwhelming public concern for the cost of education and a public outcry for accountability. Laurel Schmidt points out in her book that it is not just your community that is scrutinizing you. As a principal, you are watched by many people: state and federal legislators, special interest groups, taxpayers, the media, private enterprises, big businesses, the local business community, the board of education, your superintendent, the parents, school site governance groups, the teacher's union, and the teachers themselves.

A leader with vision, one with standards who holds the students' right to a quality education as a top priority will pass both public and private scrutiny. Your school will thrive, your teachers will be on your team, and your school community will support you in times of turmoil and tribulation. The day may come when your school falls under the microscope. Good leaders know how to deal with challenging issues and will keep their school community standing on solid ground in the eyes of the numerous concerned entities.

CHAPTER 4

Politics in Education

Control and funding for education in America comes from three places: federal, state, and local governments. The federal government sets the standards on how much money each district is allowed from federal funding, while the state has a say in how much funding certain schools will receive from state funds.

Students have the option of public schools, private schools, or home school. In public and private schools, education is divided into three levels: elementary, junior high or middle school, and high school. The process is straightforward: divide students by age groups, place them in the schools of their parents' choosing, and give them a quality education.

At the time of the 2008 American Community Survey (ACS), more than 79.9 million students were enrolled in schools across America. According to the most recent figures from the U.S. Census Bureau, the population of Americans over the age of 15 has a literacy rate of 99 percent; however, the true figure depends on one's definition of literacy. A comprehensive 2003 study released by the National Center for Education Statistics (NCES) found that one in seven U.S. adults were functionally illiterate.

In America, the first year of schooling begins at 5 or 6 years old in kindergarten, and with 13 years of education following, one would think all students would graduate high school with the ability to read and write at an appropriate level. Unfortunately, this is not always the case.

Where are schools failing the students? Why are schools failing the students? This is a concern that must weigh heavily on all principals, new and veteran alike.

Let us review some of the goals that are set for the principal by local, state, and federal departments.

No Child Left Behind

Curricular decisions vary widely in school systems across the country. Individual school systems determine public education curricula based on a state's learning standards. However, the state and the school district now mandate the standards you cover in your classroom. These standards are set so your students can better meet the level the federal government set in the No Child Left Behind Act (NCLB). In 2002, NCLB was signed into law and was passed with intentions of getting all students' performances up to their grade level by the year 2014. NCLB was created with intentions of having all students receive a quality education, regardless of race, geographic location, or nationality, and to be at a certain level of knowledge according to their grade. NCLB established an accountability system that requires each state to ensure that all state schools and districts make Adequate Yearly Progress (AYP), which was designed to show that students are improving each year.

Another provision of NCLB requires all states to test students in public schools to ensure they are receiving the minimum level of education guaranteed to them. Standardized testing originated in China during the Han dynasty with imperial examinations designed to ensure that political appointments were based on merit instead of favoritism or nepotism. These tests focused on proficiency in the "Six Arts," which included knowledge of rituals and ceremonies; music; archery and horsemanship; arithmetic; and writing.

The world's largest private educational testing and research organization, the Educational Testing Service, was established in 1947. In 1965, the Elementary and Secondary Education Act (ESEA) required standardized testing in public schools, and the NCLB Act tied the knot of public funding to standardized testing.

Each state has its own way of attaining federal requirements when it comes to NCLB. One example of this is the Ohio Achievement Test (OAT). This test is given in grades three through eight, and the test is based on Ohio's Academic Content Standards. In high school, Ohio uses the Ohio Graduation Test (OGT), which is given in tenth grade, to assess students. Those who do not pass the OAT or the OGT are allowed to retake the test, or certain sections of the test they do not pass, until all subject areas are passed. If the student does not pass all subject areas in the OGT before their graduation date, they are not allowed to receive their diploma. In Florida, the Florida Comprehensive Assessment Test

(FCAT) is administered to students in grades three through 11. This test has criteria to be met in the subject areas of math, writing, science, and reading. It is based on the Sunshine State Standards (SSS), which are benchmarks created by the state to meet the NCLB standards.

NCLB forces states to be accountable, and the accountability system is based on the development of state content and academic achievement standards. If the state wishes to receive NCLB funding, said state must meet the federal standards in reading/language arts, math, and science. The U.S. Department of Education allows each state to develop its own standards, assessments, and AYP, but said standards are reviewed by the U.S. Department of Education before and after testing.

An advantage of standardized testing is that the results can be documented and scores can be shown. This is helpful for admissions personnel in higher education when comparing students from across the nation — or the world. The disadvantage of standardized testing is that some school district leaders become tempted to have principals form curricula strictly designed to teach for the tests, just so they can receive the funding that comes with adequate test results. Test preparation is a growing concern as it is another factor in the stress level of students, which has recently become such an issue that many schools are implementing stress-reducing activities such as yoga.

There are four mainstays of the NCLB:

- Accountability
- Flexibility in federal funding

- Scientifically based educational programs
- Certain rights for parents of students

Some of the sanctions for failing to meet NCLB standards, according to the law, require schools to offer extra tutoring and allow parents to transfer their children to higher performing schools. The extra tutoring comes out of school budgets, forcing cuts elsewhere, which leads to students doing even worse on state tests. When students do poorly on the standardized tests, schools begin facing a possible state takeover, another sanction, and administrators and teachers become desperate because it will mean losing their jobs. A school board does not want an administrator who cannot get his or her school to meet the set standards.

There were once stringent rules as to how public schools could spend federal funding. With NCLB, these rules are now more relaxed. Funds may now be spent with specific needs based upon a school's locality, such as more training for teachers. If a school district has a high ratio of teachers with special needs students, training is more crucial for these teachers. Training improves staff development and is therefore justified as needed.

NCLB allows parents other alternatives if their child is attending a low-performing school. Transferring a student is allowed if the school is deemed low performing for two consecutive years. If the school is low performing for three years, the parent may remove the child and place him or her in a better performing school in the same district or receive supplemental services, such as tutoring.

In the News: President Obama's Vision for Education

There are changes on the horizon for NCLB that you need to be aware of as principal. At the time of publication, President Barack Obama was seeking to renew ESEA and proposing an overhaul of NCLB once the renewal was approved. The new proposals would change the way school success or failure is judged and would eliminate the 2014 deadline for bringing every American child up to the appropriate level academically. Although the proposed changes would eliminate many of the provisions educators have found most objectionable, the Obama administration would keep in place the act's goal of encouraging teacher equality and closing the achievement gap between white and minority students. It would also make the standards for student achievement more clearly defined and would seek to improve teacher skills.

One of the proposals is to change the way federal money is doled out: Instead of basing the numbers on a formula that portions funds to districts based on how many students they have, the administration wants to restructure the process so the schools that show academic progress are awarded. The current system, critics say, depends on what amounts to a yearly pass-fail report card, but fails to distinguish between the nuanced reasons schools may be failing: schools with persistent, deep problems; schools that are successfully helping low-scoring students improve; and schools that grade well but are ignoring the low-scoring pupils they may have. According to a February 2010 article in the *New York Times*, the current form of the law had labeled more than 30,000 schools "in need of improvement" up to that point, but the states and districts had done little or nothing to help these schools improve. The goal of the proposed reform is to develop an improved accountability system that better categorizes schools when dispensing federal funds. It would also provide more money to either help improve or close failing institutions. In place of the 2014 universal proficiency deadline, the new goal would be for all students to graduate high school "college- and career-ready."

The Obama proposal also aims to provide more flexibility for states and focuses on improving the "bottom 1 percent" of schools, Education Secretary Arne Duncan said in a White House press release. Both goals address the other main criticisms of the law. A February 2010 report by the National Conference of State Legislatures (NCSL) said that the U.S. government's interference in school curriculum and reforms in the last decade has hurt students and suggested that the federal government rescind some of that control back to the states. It also criticized NCLB for having impossible standards and inadvertently withholding much-needed funds from the schools that need it the most.

To back the proposed changes, President Obama outlined an additional $3.5 billion in federal education funding in his budget proposal for the 2011 fiscal year, $3 billion of which is specifically geared toward ESEA, the largest increase ever requested for these programs. Another $1 billion would be requested once NCLB was reauthorized.

> Given the financial crunch most states are in,
> such changes would significantly impact the way
> schools are able to deal with state budget cuts
> and still provide an optimal quality of education
> to students.

While you were attending college, you were taught that whether a school operates effectively would determine the chances of a student's academic success. This makes your involvement in curriculum, instruction, and assessment critical. It is important for you to accept the importance of the NCLB standards and make sure your teachers are adequately preparing their students for these tests.

Your knowledge of subject matter is as important as the teachers' knowledge of the same. According to a 1999 study on leadership by researchers at the National Institute on Educational Governance, Finance, Policymaking and Management, a principal's willingness to provide input on classroom practices is highly valued by teachers. Most teachers desire regular meetings with the principal, who then assesses practices and provides instructional feedback. The only way this can truly be beneficial to teachers is if you are knowledgeable in these domains. In order to meet federal, state, and local district standards, and to give the best guidance possible to your teachers, it is highly advisable for principals to have regular meetings with other administrators. This is the best way to stay aware of changes and advances in the curriculum.

CASE STUDY: WORD FROM THE EXPERTS

Thoughts on Laws and Litigation in Education

- "The laws that require the most attention usually involve issues regarding special needs situations. I do not personally have concerns, but I do work diligently to stay in compliance with the technical aspects of individual educational plans. I also try to read current law cases because you never know what might apply to you on any given day. There are people in our district office to guide me through any 'sticky' situations." — **Tammy Brown**

- "The state of Florida voted to only have a certain number of students in each class, and that causes a big problem when you have new students register, and you have to fit them in classes that you have no room for growth in." — **Katherine Munn**

- "When I have a concern about whether or not I am in compliance with state and federal law, I first turn to the Internet for answers. Our district subscribes to eLaw®, which is an online-based legal consultant. If I am still in doubt about a concern, I turn to the superintendent for suggestions. I try not to bother my superintendent unless necessary." — **Tret Witherspoon**

Some parts of a given curriculum are guaranteed, and some are simply practical. When a curriculum is guaranteed, a school is responsible for determining that classroom teachers teach specific content in specific classes for specific grade levels. There have been many arguments over why the same basic curriculum — such as math, writing, reading, and science — is not taught in each school across the nation, but the truth is that if every school used the same curriculum, it still would not be taught using the same methods. You can give every teacher the same book and require they teach the same content, but each teacher is an individual and will use different methods to teach while possibly adding to or leaving out portions of content.

This is another problem with standardized testing. If certain content in a given curriculum is mandated, how is it to be monitored? Testing shows what students are or are not learning based only on what is on the standardized tests; these tests and the content included are changed every year, so it is impossible to know what will be tested. Therefore, even if the same curriculum is mandated, it still does not guarantee that the students will be learning exactly what they will be tested on.

Mandated tests are constantly changing, evolving, and becoming more demanding. The best leaders have shown that if they ignore the anxiety over standardized test scores and simply continue to ensure that their students are receiving the best education they can possibly give them, the test scores will naturally fall into place. The most effective principals have stated they think of standardized testing as a means for improving curricula.

Every decision you make as a principal should depend on what is best for your students. It is up to you to stay abreast of what your students are learning. In small districts, the principal is usually a significant player in curriculum development. In larger districts, a principal usually sits on a curriculum committee and is expected to scrutinize stated curricula, assure the appropriate information is being taught, and verify that it is resulting in student progress. To provide the best instructional leadership, you must work with your teachers and create committees, and then, in turn, work with those committees to continually assess curricula. These discussions should lead to new ideas and improvement in teaching methods and student achievements. It is also up to you to ensure that your committees, and your teachers, are familiar with any new state mandates. Regular meetings can give you the needed time to pass this information on to them.

Inclusion

In the mid-1960s, President Lyndon B. Johnson's "Great Society" programs included the Elementary and Secondary Education Act, which was an attempt to do away with poverty and racial injustice. A decade later, the U.S. Supreme Court enacted federal legislation — the Individuals with Disabilities Education Act (IDEA) — that required states to ensure the same education for students with disabilities as those without disabilities.

After a number of federal and state laws were passed, school districts found themselves scrambling to provide services to students with exceptional needs. Bureaucratic rights have since been established protecting the rights of parents of special needs children so they have a voice in their children's education. Rights have also been established to protect the students and ensure their educational rights. What has come from these laws and rights is better known as inclusion. An inclusion classroom incorporates teaching special needs students in regular classrooms, eliminating the need for a special needs school whenever possible.

The IDEA gives the federal government the power to govern how state and public agencies provide for these children from birth to the age of 21. It ensures that students with disabilities will receive the appropriate services, including special education programs. The IDEA also requires that students be placed in the least restrictive environment (LRE), which means that schools must make all efforts to educate children with disabilities in regular classes, with any special aids or support they might need, alongside their nondisabled peers. Funds are readily available to states that comply with the minimum policies and procedures regarding the education of children with disabilities.

In 1997, amendments were made to IDEA that required schools to educate special needs children in regular classrooms whenever possible. This was when the requirement for all special needs children to have an Individual Education Program (IEP) plan was put into place. By law, the IEP must be developed by a team of people that includes teachers, administrators, parents, councilors, and outside experts, such as a psychologist who interprets the student's evaluation test and the instructional implications that will follow. The student for whom the plan is developed is also part of the IEP team. Together, this team creates a learning plan that stresses the special needs of the child so his or her educational needs are met.

Schools had to be restructured to adapt to inclusion, and today the inclusion classroom is the standard classroom model because the typical classroom now includes children with special needs. All students are entitled to the best education possible, and these special needs must be met. There are legal requirements principals must implement to comply with federal and state mandates. If they are not met, there could be legal consequences, so be sure to know the appropriate laws and be sure all procedures are followed. Such requirements may include special education programs, remedial assistance, and programs for special gifts and talents. It is important to learn all you can about a disabled student's unique educational needs so all possible and appropriate actions can be taken to meet those needs. These mandates were put into place to guarantee a free appropriate public education that will prepare students with disabilities for employment and independent living.

A student does not automatically qualify for special education services just because they have a disability. Under the IDEA, a qualifying student is defined as a child with mental retardation, hearing impairments, speech impairments, language impairments, visual impairments, serious emotional disturbance, orthopedic impairments, autism, traumatic brain injury, specific learning disabilities, and other health impairments. Section 304 of the Rehabilitation Act of 1973 protects these children. Students who do not qualify may fall under accommodations or modifications under the Americans with Disabilities Act (ADA).

Discipline of a child with disabilities is another concern. The IDEA laws provide that the disability of a student must be taken into account before disciplining said student. For example, if a child with autism rushes out of the room where there are consistently loud noises and activity, the child's sensitivity to loud noise and excessive activity must be taken into account.

The United States Department of Education (DE) states that if a child with a disability has been suspended for ten days total for each school year, the school authority must hold a hearing to determine if the child's behavior was caused by his or her disability, known as a Manifestation Determination Review (MDR), within ten school days. This hearing will take place before any decision on the placement of that student can be reached. The hearing will determine if the student's conduct in question was:

- Caused by or had a direct relationship to the child's disability

- The direct result of the local education agency's failed attempt to implement the IEP

If it is determined that the conduct was due to the child's disability, the IEP team then must:

- Implement a behavioral intervention plan.

- Review the behavioral intervention plan, and modify as necessary.

- Return the student to the placement from which he or she was removed.

Safeguards are designed to protect the rights of children with disabilities, as well as those of their families. These safeguards were placed to ensure that children with disabilities received a free, appropriate public education.

Although the government requires compliance with these mandates, it also promised funding to help ensure these restrictions could be met. Under the IDEA, the federal government is to supply up to 40 percent of the estimated excess cost to districts in educating students with disabilities. For the fiscal year of 2008, federal funding covered 17.1 percent of the excess cost of educating students with disabilities. The shortfalls in federal funding for the IDEA requirements have thus fallen to state and local governments, and states provide only a minimum basic special education allocation based on a per pupil amount for a district's entire student population. Funds for special education services are distributed through Special Education Local Plan Areas (SELPA). Under certain circumstances, charter schools also receive funds through SELPA.

How does this affect the schools? If a child who attends your school is in a wheelchair, for example, you must have wheelchair access ramps. These ramps are expensive, and the money must come from somewhere, but regardless of where it comes from, by law, it must be done. This leads to one of the criticisms of the IDEA: while it does protect students with disabilities and their families, it does not protect districts, schools, and teachers.

Another special needs area is for English learners, more commonly referred to as English as a Second Language (ESL) students. The U.S. Supreme Court established English Language Learners (ELL) rights by passing the Equal Educational Opportunity Act of 1974. School districts are now required to address linguistic deficiencies of language minorities. Unfortunately, the court failed to suggest any specific way in which the schools are to remedy the problem.

Through all of these state and federal requirements you must meet, bear in mind that your faculty is there to help you succeed. Your success is their success, and all of you are working together to achieve the same goal.

The Watchful Eyes Upon You

Education is in a perpetual state of reform. Groups of outsiders will make decisions for your school on everything from which textbooks your teachers will use to what your budget will be. John Redd stated the obvious quite eloquently: "Politicians want to be the watchdogs of education; they just do not want to take the blame when the proper funding is not there."

There are many people watching and observing the outcome of your students with keen interest. Although you may have only the slightest notion that these watchers exist, it is best to know they are there and why. Those interested parties include:

- State and federal legislatures
- Special interest groups
- Taxpayers
- The media
- Private enterprise
- Big business
- Local business community
- Board of education
- Your superintendent
- Parents
- School-site governance groups
- Teachers' union
- Teachers

"Schools are sometimes the scapegoat of our society."

Barry Pichard, principal
Sunrise Elementary School
Palm Bay, Florida

Many groups benefit politically from your success or failure. The following sections detail each of these watchers and discuss how they relate to the education sector.

State and federal legislatures

Before campaigning, politicians will take notice of what concerns their constituents have, and during their campaigns, they will assure the people they have a solution to these concerns, and they will implement said solutions as soon as they are voted into office. Once they are voted into office, they make new laws that the schools, and you as principal, must abide by.

"The media in the U.S. is overwhelmingly committed to big government, gun control, and the supremacy of state-controlled education over parent-controlled education," said political consultant and lecturer Michael I. Rothfeld. This is an issue for many parents, because government officials often do not really understand the true workings of a school — how curriculum is assessed, chosen, and implemented, for instance.

One shining example, though, is the former governor of North Carolina, James Hunt. During his four terms as governor, Hunt applauded the efforts of good educational leaders and stressed the importance of a good education. Now he runs the James B. Hunt, Jr. Institute for Educational Leadership and Policy, established in 2001, a nonprofit agency affiliated with the University of North Carolina formed to educate governors, state leaders, and other political, business, and educational leaders on scholastic policy. The Hunt Institute was created to help such leaders formulate ways to implement strategies and make legal changes to improve educational programs. According to the RAND Corporation, North Carolina public schools improved test scores more than any other state in the 1990s, during Hunt's tenure.

Special interest groups

These groups lobby the politicians, donate large amounts of money, and finance candidates who run for the school boards. These groups pressure politicians and school board candidates to do something, anything, to aid or alleviate their special interest, which may include students with disabilities, cultural problems in communities, racial issues, school vouchers, sex education, health education, obese students, anorexic students, and gender issues.

Taxpayers

Even those who have no children in school must pay taxes that are used for the schools. This is true for most cities, towns, villages, and communities. Because of this, people rightfully want to know where and how their money is being spent.

The media

Newspapers and television media alike have a responsibility to report all information relevant to their respective communities. This includes news both good and bad in relation to your school. Unfortunately, the negative usually receives more attention than the positive, especially on a national scale. The media has a huge influence on how communities see their schools. Always be prepared, because the media is always watching for a story.

Private enterprise

These enterprises move in when schools are failing and decentralize control from district offices. The control is then taken by an organization such as EdisonLearning Inc., a group that partners with school districts to create innovative programs to help students reach their potential.

Big business

Numerous businesses publish and distribute standardized tests, textbooks, data-processing services, and test preparation materials. If a school is not performing adequately, it will usually try new curricula that require new textbooks. If students are not doing well on standardized tests, these businesses will publicize their materials so schools purchase said materials to help students achieve higher scores.

Local business community

Schools with higher achieving students are assets for local businesses. Being able to claim one of the best schools in the region makes it easier for the chamber of commerce, Rotary, real estate agents, and city councils to attract new businesses, sell homes, and entice new members of the community, who will then pay city taxes. The local business community likes to see local schools with successful students due to its stake in education. Not only does this attract potential job candidates, but schools that have excellent students also graduate candidates for future employment.

The board of education

School board members have an interest in successful students for various reasons. Many board members will remain citizens of the community and work for the school board as long as they are re-elected. Their interest comes from a personal investment, as well as an aversion to e-mails and phone calls from disgruntled parents. The school board also has the worry of negative media attention, just as you do.

The superintendent

The average time for a superintendent to stay with one school district is a bit more than three years. Some superintendents will move on when a majority of new school board members are voted in or there has become a conflict of beliefs in how the school should be run. It is not uncommon for a superintendent to resign or be fired in the middle of his or her contract, and this sometimes leads to payment without service, adding to the drain on the school district's budget.

Parents

A good principal realizes the value of the parents' opinions on how the school is run. Parents can affect not only the job of the principal, but also the re-election of a school board and the money that is given to the school, depending on the level of involvement.

School-site governance groups

These are school-based management groups that usually consist of administrators, principals, teachers, parents, and other community members who make decisions at each school site. They have control over the budget and school improvements, and sometimes they have subcommittees that find new curricula or debate the hiring of new staff members, for example.

Teachers' unions

Unions are good in many ways, but sometimes they can also cause problems. Although they do a good job representing teachers, they also hinder the firing of tenured personnel whose performances have become unsatisfactory.

Teachers

These are the people who hold the most power to ensure educational success for your students, but they are usually the last people to know of reforms taking place in the schools. Often, teachers may refrain from being involved in such matters unless it is due to self-preservation.

With so many eyes watching your progress or failure, you are sure to feel the pain of such scrutiny at some time in your career. Just remember there are parents and students who respect what you do every day, and understand the complexities of your job, the burdens you must carry, and the scarce recognition you receive for your accomplishments.

CASE STUDY: WORD FROM THE EXPERTS

Advice on Dealing with The Watchful Eyes

- "News media loves a good story. I can attest to that. One day, early on in my new role, we had a problem with the water, and the toilets did not flush. We had trucks of water being shipped in, bottled water for drinking, and luckily, it was an early release day. Instead of the news media focusing on what the cause was or how the community may have rallied to our aide, they chose to take pictures of the dirty toilets." — **Tammy Brown**

- "Anyone that's on the outside looking in is eager to exert his or her two cents in. All politicians should spend a couple of weeks in a school to get an inside perspective of the day-to-day operation of a school." — **Tret Witherspoon**

- "Schools, especially public schools, are constantly under the microscope. Lawmakers often use data in a way that is not always comprehensible to schools' personnel, but it may be to the public, especially during an election year. In our area, we have a large population of retirees who are always looking for ways to cut taxes, and often lowering school taxes is something that gets votes. Most of us wish we could make the retirees understand that if you don't pay for education first, you will pay for it later, with building more prisons." — **Barbara Belanger**

- "My goal is to always be transparent to what we are doing. That takes a lot of speculating away from the media." — **Michael Miller**

- "Have an open-door policy for yourself and for the school. Invite politicians, the media, and parents to spend time at the school to observe first-hand the challenges educators face everyday. This will usually diffuse critics once they see first-hand what educators contend with on a daily basis." — **Leonard Weiss**

In the News: Race to the Top

The Obama administration, at the time of publication, is working to find ways to ease the burden for teachers and at the same time improve the quality of education the students receive. President Obama attempted to begin this process through the American Recovery and Reinvestment Act of 2009. On the official website of the Department of Education (www.ed.gov), it stated, "Providing a high quality education for all children is critical to America's economic future." The site went on to state that President Obama is "committed to providing every child access to a complete and competitive education, from cradle through career."

The American Recovery and Reinvestment Act provided the following funds:

- $5 billion for early learning programs, including programs for children with special needs

- $77 billion for reforms to strengthen elementary and secondary education, including $48.6 billion to stabilize state education budgets

- $5 billion in competitive funds to spur innovation

In the American Recovery and Reinvestment Act, $77 billion was earmarked for reform to strengthen elementary and secondary education; this allotment was also to be used to encourage states to "make improvements in teacher effectiveness and ensure that all schools have highly qualified teachers." In February 2009, President Obama signed into law provisions of $98.2 billion in funding for the Department of Education.

On November 4, 2009, the White House released a statement on President Obama's commitment to reforming America's public schools. The release said he was presenting states with an "unprecedented challenge and the opportunity to compete in a 'Race to the Top' designed to spur systemic reform and innovative approaches to teaching and learning in America's schools." The Race to the Top challenge is backed by $4.3 billion dollars and expands effective support to teachers and principals. Instead of just splitting up the funds and handing them out, the Obama administration devised this form of competition to inspire principals, teachers, and school boards to reach create solutions for improvements in teacher skills and student achievement.

"What we're saying here is, if you can't decide to change these practices, we're not going to use precious dollars that we want to see creating better results; we're not going to send those dollars there," Obama told *The Washington Post* in a July 2009 interview. "And we're counting on the fact that, ultimately, this is an incentive, this is a challenge for people who do want to change."

What this ultimately means is that the schools that show the dedication to reform will be the ones that earn the grants, and those that do not meet the requirements will not receive any of these funds; it is also voluntary, so any school or district that does not wish to participate does not have to do so. Part of the goal of the competition is to ease limits on charter schools as well as tie teachers' salaries to student achievement. The former pillar of President Obama's aim with this initiative caused some concern among the educator population, as teachers were already incredibly critical of the NCLB system labeling them and their students as failures through test scores.

But in his speech announcing the grant program, President Obama said, "This is not about the kind of testing that has mushroomed under No Child Left Behind. This is not about more tests. It's not about teaching to the test. And it's not about judging a teacher solely on the results of a single test."

According to a White House press release, Race to the Top emphasizes:

- Devising and employing high-quality standards and assessments

- Attracting and keeping great teachers in class-rooms across the country

- Using data to make decisions regarding how to improve education

- Using innovative and effective approaches to improve struggling schools

- Demonstrating and sustaining education reform

Forty states and the District of Columbia submit-ted applications for the first part of the chal-lenge with a January 2010 deadline, with the win-ners to be announced in April 2010; a later deadline for the remaining applications was set for June 2010, with the winners announced in September 2010. Thus, the funds will be awarded in two waves.

At the first deadline, President Obama announced a continuation of the challenge due to the overwhelming response and requested $1.35 billion for the program in his 2010-2011 budget proposal.

As a principal, you may be involved with plans for Race for the Top or new programs or standards in conjunction with an award of the grant. It is your duty to ensure that the funds are properly used to improve the quality of your teachers and the achievement of your students.

In the News: Budget Cuts

Many governors, senators, congressional representatives, and presidents have run their campaigns on improving education in our states. However, as soon as the economy takes a downward turn, one of the first sectors to experience cuts is education. This is a worrisome trend for an area already maligned with financial hardship, and it has only gotten worse with the current state of the economy.

In 2006, President Bush proposed to cut education spending by more than $3 billion dollars, but at the same time, he wanted to strengthen math and science programs. Many of the budget cuts came from scrapping education programs for the arts and state grants for vocational education, but in his State of the Union address, Bush spoke of his focus on math and science in creating the American Competitiveness Initiative. This initiative included $250 million dollars for elementary programs to boost math achievement.

The Obama administration's $787 billion federal stimulus package, which was designed to spark the economy and slow unemployment rates, helped ease these cuts and took some of the pressure off of the state and local governments by providing roughly $100 billion for education. Of those funds, $54 million was designed to ease the financial strain on state budgets. Obama said in his initial State of the Union that the stimulus created or saved roughly 300,000 education jobs.

But those stimulus funds are running out for many states, and the budget problems they faced beforehand remain, leading state governments to slash spending on education even more. A January 2010 report by the Center on Budget and Policy Priorities found that 41 states were facing midyear budget deficiencies of $35 billion. The school districts, in turn, are forced to cut programs; lay off teachers and staff members; decrease paychecks and supplemental income; gash electives, after-school activities, and summer-school programs; and expand class sizes to make up for money lost from state funding. According to a February article from the Associated Press, experts said the looming cuts would weaken the public school system, worsen unemployment, undermine Obama's education vision, and widen the gap of achievement in rich and poor districts.

In Michigan, which has the highest unemployment rate in the country, school districts lost 2 percent of state funds in 2010 and faced potential further cuts of 4 percent in 2011. Gov. Jennifer Granholm proposed an incentive program to try to entice 39,000 public school employees to retire to close the budgeting gap

Washington state school districts lost $1.7 billion in state money from 2008 to 2010, and with a $2.8 billion state deficit for the 2010-2011 fiscal year, districts planned on overhauling the bus routes to make them more efficient, increasing class sizes even more, laying off nonunion staff members, and implementing a hiring freeze. But in a February 4, 2010 decision, King County Superior Court Judge John Erlick found the state in violation of its constitution in regard to school funding. The document proclaims education to be the "paramount" duty of the state, and the suit held that the state was falling short in its fiscal responsibility to the schools. In McCleary v. Washington State, also known as the Network for Excellence in Washington Schools lawsuit, Erlick ordered the state's legislature to determine the actual full cost of providing each student a basic education; the legislature must then implement a new system to ensure that the districts have the funding they need.

In Virginia, Gov. Bob McDonnell proposed a cut of $731 million in K-12 funds over 2010-2012 to help cover a $2 billion budgetary gap over the same period. These cuts were in addition to the $1.2 billion in cuts proposed by the state's former governor, Tim Kaine, before he left office. Districts were already closing facilities, laying off teachers and support staff, and shutting down programs in response to Kaine's cuts. But McDonnell's plan would ax several programs covered by lottery funds — including a new-teacher mentorship program — and eliminate supplemental pay for coaches, club advisors, and department or program chairs. The proposal would also reduce funds for support staff and health insurance coverage for teachers.

Nevada faced a hole of $880 million in its budget, which led Gov. Jim Gibbons to propose cuts totaling $200 million for K-12 education for the biennium ending June 30, 2011. According to the AP, Assembly Speaker Barbara Buckley, D-Las Vegas, said this would lead to thousands of teacher layoffs and high school classes of 50 students. The plan would also do away with state laws on class sizes and full-day kindergarten.

In California, thousands of teachers had already lost their jobs, while class sizes increased and academic programs were cut. State officials told the AP the outlook was even worse because most of the stimulus money was gone. Per-pupil spending was cut by 4 percent in 2009, and it would be cut by another 8 percent under Gov. Arnold Schwarzenegger's proposed 2010-2011 budget. According to the AP, the school districts laid off many teachers and guidance counselors, increased class sizes, and eliminated art and music programs. These measures would cut even deeper with the proposed slash in funds.

Florida hoped to ease some of the financial stress on public schools with an amendment to its constitutional limit on class sizes, which schools were struggling to balance with slashed budgets. The current law currently limits classes to 18 students through third grade, 22 students per class in grades four through eight, and 25 students in high school classes. Districts were also coping by closing schools during break periods, decreasing energy spending, and changing bus routes.

In Utah, a Republican state senator, Chris Buttars, proposed eliminating 12th grade to save money. According to ABC News, Buttars said making high school three years instead of four would save the state $102 million each year, money he said was being wasted on students who spent the grade doing "nothing but playing around." After his suggestion was met with harsh criticism, the senator backed down somewhat, reforming his plan to make 12th grade optional instead of cutting it out entirely. Buttars' proposal also included the elimination of bussing for high school students, which he said would save $15 million.

Minnesota school districts also sought to reduce spending on gas for school buses, but instead of cutting bussing completely, they took a route that has grown in popularity with many rural school districts — shaving the school week from five days to four.

These are just some of the many states facing budget crises, which makes it quite possible that you will be dealing with situations and cuts similar to those listed above in your first year as principal. It is important that you involve your teachers in discussions on how to cope with such difficulties; the only way to ensure that your students are still getting the education they deserve is for you and your faculty to work together to find solutions to the problems these financial limitations will present. It is likely your classes will be larger than you or your teachers would prefer, for instance, but if you have no other options, you need to discuss as a group the best way to make it work so your students are still learning and succeeding.

CHAPTER 5

Communication

The duties of a principal are innumerable. The role of leader comes with many burdens. Student success is only part of it. In your daily duties, you will talk with students, teachers, parents, the community, and the media. All of these dealings require exceptional communication skills. You must understand the correct way to speak with each type of individual and how to navigate potentially messy situations, such as teacher conflicts and student discipline. You should also be prepared as the leader of your school to communicate with the members of your community through the media. Though your responsibilities are endless, this chapter is focused on helping you prepare for future situations.

"As a public school administrator, there is no room for designer heels."

Pamela Mitchell, principal
Central Middle School
West Melbourne, Florida

Developing the Lines of Communication

Once you are an authority figure, as a principal is viewed, you may find that some teachers are not completely forthcoming in communication. In their eyes, you are not a peer or an equal, but the boss. How do you maintain the lines of communication without losing your role as leader? The answer is to be respectful of others at all times. Think of how you would prefer an authority figure to approach you and communicate with teachers in a similar fashion.

If you make coming to work a pleasant experience rather than a dreaded chore, teachers will love you for it. If you create an atmosphere that is pleasant to work in, teachers will enjoy working for you. If you give recognition when it is deserved, your staff will follow you anywhere you go. Praise your teachers for the outstanding work they do. If you commend a teacher with each newsletter you send to parents, for instance, you will boost morale and create a buzz in the community. By acknowledging praiseworthy efforts, you are communicating your vision and inviting the teachers to become part of your team.

There are many obstacles for a first-year principal, but none that cannot be overcome. All things are possible if you keep the lines of communication strong and positive. As with all organizations, the success of a school depends on communication and information. Keeping your staff and personnel on the same page is essential, and there are many ways to do this. Memos, meetings, e-mails, committees, and bulletin boards are just a few ways of maintaining communication. However, face-to-face meetings are essential in building relationships and trust. One-on-one conversations are a good way to let your teachers know you are not there to tell them how to do their jobs, but to help them do their jobs. Never forget that informed teachers are happy teachers.

It is inevitable that there will be occasions when personal problems will affect the work of your teachers. When they come to you with such dilemmas, they may be seeking guidance or simply a sympathetic ear. A caring leader will listen out of concern for your staff and your school. If possible, help the teacher find a solution that will not negatively affect his or her performance at work.

It is important to realize, however, that you cannot and should not take on the personal problems of your staff. There is a fine line between listening as a leader and listening to gripes and complaints that have no effect on the job of staff members. Be sure to draw the line early so your time and energy are not unnecessarily wasted.

In our fast-paced society, technology is constantly changing, and this is a good place to start when searching for ways to implement change. Encourage teachers to attend seminars, classes, or training programs aimed at personal growth and professional development. To approach the issue, find a way to make the idea inviting rather than a forceful suggestion. You could try to find humor in the situation or give them a reason to look forward to learning something new.

In the News: Education Technology

As technology develops and improves, schools must continually change and adapt to keep up. Given the popularity of cell phones and iPods® with students, schools are starting to use these mobile devices as teaching tools. Educators are beginning to embrace the concept that students can learn anywhere and anytime. The Virginia Department of Education began an initiative in 2008 called Learning without Boundaries to study, in conjunction with Virginia Tech and Radford University, the possible benefits of wireless mobile handheld technologies for day-to-day teaching in schools. Some educators feel such devices would cause problems with cheating and "sexting," one of the reasons many schools implementing such programs purchase the devices as property of their school district.

Another inventive way schools are trying to promote on-the-go learning is through installing Wi-Fi routers for mobile Internet access on buses, which allows students to use their laptop computers on the bus ride to and from school. This experiment effectively turns the buses into mobile Internet cafés, quieting what can often be rambunctious rides and increasing student productivity. Although such "Internet buses" are currently limited in number, the company marketing these routers, Autonet Mobile, has sold them to schools and districts in Florida, Missouri, Arizona, and Washington D.C., according to a February article in the *New York Times*.

These are just two examples of the ways current advances in technology are being implemented in the education realm. Other schools offer advanced online classes, videoconference lectures or lessons, and eBooks or laptops, instead of textbooks. The students of today connect with technology, and the motivation to use such devices is a powerful way to increase learning and productivity. It is important for you as a principal to ensure that your school takes advantage of the technology available to it.

Not only is it important your teachers get consistent opportunities for professional development, it is a formula for disaster if they do not. Education is like a pool of water. If the water is unmoving and no fresh water is ever added, it becomes stagnant and eventually grows infested with disease-ridden bacteria. Education is the same. If teachers do not grow or develop professionally, their teaching methods will become stale and outdated, which in turn means the students will not succeed and flourish.

Vision and teamwork are two elements that should take place in your school every day, and a good way to get new teachers on board with these two imperative elements is to create a committee of veteran teachers to guide them. By doing this, you are simultaneously recognizing the skills of your veteran teachers and welcoming new teachers into the fold.

Teachers and principals alike dread boring staff meetings. Rather than being used to recognize the work done by teachers on a daily basis or ask for their priceless input, these meetings are normally dry, dull, and fruitless. You, as principal, have the power to make it a practice your teachers look forward to. Ask your teachers for their opinion on staff meetings, and you might be surprised by the negativity. Ask for their suggestions on how to make the meetings an asset, and you may receive invaluable feedback.

For your first staff meeting, develop a plan that will motivate your staff and boost its morale — you will find a room full of passionate and creative adults. Teachers develop projects for their students. They put ideas into motion, and they can do the same for one another. Put the meetings into the hands of the teachers, asking them to determine a goal and develop ideas to achieve that goal. As a result, you will find your load as a leader considerably lighter.

Communication is as important as the selection of words is powerful. Always choose your wording carefully because if you do not, your staff may interpret your message incorrectly. When you first explain your expectations to your teachers, you must do so diplomatically, but also clearly. You do not want teachers walking out of your first meeting with the impression that your expectations are merely suggestions.

There are so many ways to communicate with people today that it can be overwhelming. There are faxes, letters, e-mails, instant messages, and voice-mail messages. These are all forms of contact that you, as a leader, cannot afford to ignore. You must also acknowledge any handwritten notes, sticky notes, phone calls, beepers, walkie-talkies, and face-to-face meetings. With all these forms of communication, you might wonder how you will find the time to walk the halls to observe and build relationships with your students and teachers.

The best way to deal with all these forms of communication is to pick a day to answer them, unless of course, it is an emergency.

You may also wish to limit what is public. Your e-mail address can be private or restricted to certain people. Silence your voice mail and answer it only at the end of the day. Restrict phone calls to certain school hours. Instant messaging should probably be kept personal, and phone messages can be handled in priority form at the discretion of your secretary. As long as your time is spent with your students' best interest as the priority, there are few who will find fault in your decision to limit forms of communication.

It has been said that 30 to 40 percent of a principal's time is spent dealing with conflict. This may include conflicts between teachers and students, principals and students, parents and teachers, teachers and principals, and community troubles that involve the schools. You are the leader, you make the decisions, and the resolution of each conflict rests in your lap.

Unfortunately, times of crisis or acts of violence may arise. According to a 2008 study released by the NCES, the most recent figures available, there were 55 violent deaths, including 40 homicides, at elementary and secondary schools between July 2006 and June 2007. These figures do not include injuries in school bus or car accidents, school-related sexual abuse cases, drug-related illnesses or deaths, or physical and emotional bullying and abuse. Due to these inexhaustible incidents, you would be well advised to have a crisis management team. This team should have regular meetings to decide how best to handle given situations. Establishing and practicing operational procedures for possible crises is essential, but no matter how often the team meets or how many situations they try to prepare for, every imaginable crisis is different, and the factors that are involved in each circumstance will differ as well. Possibilities can be planned for, but every possible scenario cannot.

Another problem in the schools is the number of organizations wanting to test new programs in the schools. "Everyone uses the schools as their own training area," said Barry Pichard. "Even the local politicians, police, fire, environmental groups, civic organizations, all have a school component of an essay, poetry, poster, banner, public speaking, et cetera, to get the schools involved in their effort or organization."

There are always "special programs" being brought to the schools by organizations, interrupting class time and learning time. Gun control, bullying, sexual harassment, and character education are just a few of the subjects Pichard has been approached about. Although many of these programs are helpful, some may be more of a distraction or interruption.

"Schools and the districts need to do a better job of screening all these requests so the teachers can do their job in teaching the students," said Pichard, "Yes, many of these are important causes, but many of them are time-consuming and are poorly organized, which is frustrating to the teaching staff, students, and parents."

In order to maintain good relations with community organizations, school districts welcome these special programs into the schools without much thought to the interruption and possible disruption of class time. When these programs are accepted into your schools by the higher administration, you, as a principal, may experience some frustration. As always, it will be up to you to make these special visits fit into the curriculum as smoothly as possible to sustain good communications with the community.

CASE STUDY: WORD FROM THE EXPERTS

The Importance of Mutual Respect

CLASSIFIED CASE STUDIES — directly from the experts

- **Tammy Brown** believes mutual respect is "extremely important, because with mutual respect comes trust. In our world, we need to rely on one another and be able to be innovating and try new things. Without trust, that can be quite difficult. I need my staff to trust that I will make the best decisions possible and that I respect their opinions as professionals. I cannot be in all places at all times, and I need to trust and respect teachers and know that they are following through on our school goals and doing what is best for children."

- "I feel as though mutual respect is vital in achieving goals in successfully managing an educational institution. Your staff will not respect you if you do not respect them. All deserve to be respected. The philosophy goes with any leadership role."
— **Tret Witherspoon**

Your Community and Public Relations

To be a good principal, you must be a people person. The majority of your time will be spent interacting with people from all stations in life: parents, students, teachers, administrative supervisors, businesspeople, staff members, vendors, and community members. There will be times when you are asked to speak at special functions and events. These occasions are important, as your presence represents the school as a whole. In order to do this successfully, you will need to know your community.

Your community is made up of the parents, the administrative supervisors (such as the school board members and the superintendent), and other members of the neighborhood including retired people, individuals or couples with no children, college students, and business personnel. In order to understand your school better, you need to understand the community and learn exactly what their expectations are for the school. Most of these community members want to have input on where their tax dollars are disbursed, which includes tax money procured for the education sector. You will find that certain groups have specific expectations. Your supervisors expressed their expectations to you when you were hired and expect you to follow through. Parents expect their children to be safe and well educated. The remainder of your community may serve on a school committee council, which many districts implement in order to provide them with an outlet to express their concerns and suggestions.

In considering these varying expectations, you will need to determine if they are feasible, taking into account each group's outlook separately and together. If it is not possible, then it is up to you to find a way to convince one or more of the groups to change or alter their expectations; otherwise, you will lose their support and can expect conflict in the future.

When mingling with the people of your new community, maintain a positive attitude throughout. Smile and greet them, introducing yourself and asking questions about them personally and the area in general. Observe how they react to you and listen to what they have to say. Invite them to school functions and events, assuring that they are welcome to visit the school and see the school community in action.

You will also want to know the history of the school and if there was — or is — an effect on the community due to the school's history. Due to financial hardships, some schools have been forced to merge in the past years, and this often creates opposing factions, both inside the school and in the community, between the merged institutions. You want to discover whether there have been school-community issues, either resolved or unresolved. If the school has a bad reputation within the community, try to find out what the reputation is built on — facts, bad public relations, or gossip. The best places to gather this information are in your backyard: churches, hair salons and barber shops, grocery stores, hardware stores, gas stations, restaurants, and even the floral shops. People love to talk once you get them to open up, and if you manage to make that happen, you will gather more information than you ever dreamed possible. Visit these places and learn the customs, beliefs, and concerns of the people. Go to the markets, the malls, local eateries, and ball games, so you can mingle with your neighbors. The best way to get along with people and gain their support is to get to know them.

You will need to look at the school district and figure out where the money comes from. Are there more parents in the community than there are senior citizens? Even if the majority of people are parents, is there a large percentage of senior citizens? If so, how could you get them involved with your school? If the parents have been shut out and turned away over the years, how can you gain their trust and get them involved with their children's education? Are there ethnic groups in your community, and are the students from those groups being educated accordingly? Are you now living in a blue-collar town or a white-collar city?

These are questions you will want to answer in order to do your job appropriately. Community plays a big part in how the schools fare, so it is up to you to get to know your community's needs and expectations.

You should also become acquainted with the community leaders. Find out if the town or city is run by a mayor, city council, charter, or another type of city government. Visit the local chamber of commerce, introduce yourself, and explain your vision for the school. Let the people of your community know you want only what is best for your students and their future.

In a small community in Ohio, the schools used to send a letter home before the teacher-parent conferences. The letter suggested that parents who had good students should not make an appointment with the teachers, thereby leaving time for parents and teachers who were having difficulties with their students. How do you think this made the parents of good students feel? Although it is understandable that problem students require more time for teachers and parents to confer, it is not a good idea to turn away the parents of students who excel. Even if the parents just want to schedule an appointment to tell the teachers thank you for doing a good job, you are taking away time those parents want and deserve, and you are taking away from the gratitude your teachers may seldom hear from parents. If you as a principal feel there is a need for more time for teacher-parent conferences to develop a plan to help students who are misbehaving or pulling bad grades, perhaps consider scheduling multiple nights for parents to come in and meet with the teachers. By pushing away parents of either kind of student, you are creating bad community relations.

One practice to consider is to hold days when parents and the community are invited as visitors to sit in during class and observe. You could do this on special occasions, such as a day when the woodshop class is building something special for the school or the oceanography class is setting up a new aquarium.

A good place to get ideas for parent and community involvement is at PTO/PTA meetings. You could ask to speak at one of the meetings and garner ideas for involving the community with the school. Just letting the members know you want the community involved will build a good foundation for future relations with your community.

You can do many things as a principal to get your community involved with the schools. The days of picnics and school fairs have almost completely vanished, but there are many communities that would love to see their school district bring those times of school-community relations back. If you decide to do something of this nature, you should invite the entire community, not just the parents or families. This is the best way to get the community involved with the schools — by inviting them to do so. You could post flyers, have the local newspaper write an article on what you are doing and why, and place invitations at the local library. The time and effort will be well worth it.

In working with the community and involving them in the school, you are using wise public relations tactics. Many clubs and organizations are more than happy to work with the schools: Kiwanis, Rotary, Lions Clubs, and First Book are just a few examples. Local businesses also like to be involved with schools, as it is good public relations for them as well. Seek out local businesses who would like to become partners with your school and help in volunteering, providing resources, and contributing monetarily. Many businesses and organizations feel a sense of pride in being involved with the local schools, and many often employ parents of the students who attend these schools, which makes the relationship between school and business all the more personal.

Letter writing is another form of good public relations. This is almost a lost art, and few administrators take the time to do it. Now, with e-mail and fax machines, communication has become cold and impersonal. By writing a letter, you let the recipient know they are important enough for you to take the time to write the letter, address the envelope, and put it with the mail to be delivered. Anytime you can communicate through a letter, it is in your best interest to do so. Even form letters are more personal than e-mails or faxes. Newsletters are a type of form letter, but the communities love to receive them, as they keep them informed about what is happening in their children's education.

You may want to consider teaching your staff public relations and communication skills as well. Regardless of how many ways you find to communicate with the community, informal communication is normally what stands out. Therefore, having your teachers and staff learn good communication skills is in your best interest. Surveys indicate that most information that is passed along is gathered from school employees. Without effective public relations, you are not going to have good school-community relations and community support.

If you are not already, be sure to keep the community informed of programs, special events, activities, and other school functions.

Make the school calendar public by placing it on the school's website and in newsletters. Many newspapers welcome the submission of a list detailing school events because they can use this information as filler on slow news days. You should also provide details such as staff information, emergency closing information, parent associations and contacts, homework policies, the school's schedule, procedures for registration, testing dates and programs available to students, and discipline policies.

In order to maintain a good relationship with your community and have good public relations with your neighborhood, you must first begin to establish one inside your school. The best place to start would probably be with your parent-teacher organizations or associations. By letting these parents know you are willing and want to work with them, you are opening doors to good relationships, and word of this will spread. If you can, it would be advisable to meet with the president of the committee before each monthly meeting, or at least quarterly. Even if you have a teacher to represent the school and attend the meetings, it is still advisable for you to meet with them personally every so often.

Being visible in your community is the first step in becoming accepted as part of it, inside the school and out. If you are visible, it says you are also available. Obviously, you cannot always be available at the drop of a hat, but when parents or community members come calling unexpectedly, it is advisable that you make yourself available if possible. If not, it is important that your office staff knows to relay this message and explain that you will be more than happy to meet with them if they schedule an appointment.

Another approach to try is calling parents to share good news about their child. If a child is chosen to receive a presidential award, what better way to find out than to have the principal call to deliver the good news? It will take all of three minutes to make the call, and that is three minutes well spent. Imagine, if you will, how many phone calls that parent will make after you hang up. Then imagine how many people that parent will relay this story to at the grocery store, the hair salon, and at his or her job.

Above all, have your staff help you keep a positive attitude inside your school as well as outside the building. The more positive you and the staff are, the more positive the students will be, and the domino effect will continue on to the parents and the rest of the community.

A parent-teacher organization in a small, rural school in Ohio devised a plan with the teachers and would visit a few classrooms every two weeks, taking candid photos of the students in action with their teachers. These photographs were developed and put on the bulletin board in the main hallway by the school entrance, and the idea was a smashing success. The students loved seeing their pictures, and the teachers, the principal, the parents, and even the superintendent enjoyed seeing the smiling faces of the students while in their school environment. Something as simple as this can boost morale 110 percent and makes for good community and public relations.

"Be open and honest. Be careful! Some reporters are just looking for a negative story. If you find someone like this, then avoid them."

Robert Spano, principal
Mike Davis Elementary School, Naples, Florida

The Media

A crisis management team seems to be the normal thought pattern for most schools since the mass shooting at Columbine High School in 1999, but no matter how carefully you plan, you can never prevent every possible threat. When horrible and senseless incidents take place, the media will be all over you, your school, your students, your staff, and the parents. Reporters will be looking for that money quote or tidbit that can be printed in the headlines for days, weeks, or perhaps even months.

Due to the fierce drive for shocking news, when a crisis does erupt, it would be in your school's best interest to have an idea of how you and your staff will handle the situation.

Chapters 1 and 2 touched on how important it is for you to become familiar with your building. It is strongly advisable that you know the layout of your building before school starts, if possible. If, by chance, you start the job in the middle of the year, get to know the building as soon as possible. In addition to knowing every inch of the building, you also want to know the grounds and all surrounding buildings.

If your school already has a crisis plan in place, learn it — all of it. Know it inside and out, backward and forward, and walk the buildings and the grounds with the crisis plan in hand. It is also a good idea to walk the buildings and grounds with a blueprint in hand. Learn every light and light switch. Know which alarms exist and where every one of them is located. Another important factor to bear in mind is the location of your fire extinguishers, the evacuation routes, and the location of all building shelters.

Obviously, you want to know all of these things for the safety and security of your students and staff, but there is another reason to have this knowledge. You will want to know all of these measures of security by heart because of the media as well.

Imagine this scenario, if you will. You are at a state-mandated meeting and, as usual, the most boring speaker was saved for last. You have been sitting in silent misery for five hours and the lot of you, teachers and principals alike, has finally been released. You are mingling, allowing the blood to circulate in your legs, sharing jokes, and laughing with a few members of your staff. A young, self-assured man approaches confidently and joins in the discussion. You notice he is wearing one of the familiar name tags just like the one that has irritated you all day, but you cannot make out his name or district due to the tag having flipped over. The discussion turns to a recent school shooting in another state. The crisis ended badly due to human error. In the middle of the conversation, this young man leans over and asks, "You are a principal, aren't you? How you would have handled the situation? How would you have evacuated your students?"

If you do not do your homework, you will end up looking like a fish out of water, flopping on the shore in total confusion. However, this is your scenario, so say you did your homework and you do know your stuff. You take a deep breath and confidently spout off the most effective crisis plan for this type of incident, relaying how you would effectively handle such an emergency, and how your students and staff would evacuate the building or lock down and stay put. Later, as the young man prepares to leave, he reaches out to shake your hand and his name tag flips over to reveal he is a reporter for a local newspaper.

This is but one example of how fast a story can turn into a possible disaster for any school or school leader. In the above scenario, you handled the situation impeccably; however, if you had not been prepared to answer the reporter's question, it would reflect badly on your school. This is why it is imperative you know your school inside and out.

Another suggestion is that you take the time to meet the police captain and the fire chief. They are remarkable assets to your community, and they are your partners in ensuring the safety of your school. A good way to establish a relationship is to pay them a scheduled visit and ask if they would personally take the time to go over the crisis plans and evacuation routes with you. This not only begins a new and important relationship in your community, but it helps you ascertain the safety of your students and staff. The input and knowledge from fire and police leaders is invaluable. If you can get them to attend a crisis management meeting, you have gained priceless information and advice.

As a first-year principal, be forewarned that an occurrence at another school — be it a school shooting, the molestation of a student, or a misunderstanding that causes a student to be expelled erroneously — could cause you to become swamped with calls or e-mails from parents and the local papers of your district.

Barry Pichard is familiar with such a scenario. He explained how such an incident happened to him: "Another Sunrise Elementary

School in Florida had a student who brought a knife to eat her lunch. At that school, they suspended the student, and it went on TV with the news report. A few days later, I get these interesting e-mails from concerned citizens condemning my school for disciplining this student."

Being a veteran principal who is aware of the importance of public relations and the backlash that could take place if the e-mails went unanswered, Pichard went on to say, "I did respond to all the concerned citizens, letting them know that they had selected the wrong Sunrise [Elementary School]. I told them the positive things about our school and also CC'd my superintendent, area superintendent, and the public relations director."

Not only did Pichard take the time to respond to the citizens, but he also kept the administration informed of what had happened, and how he had handled the situation. This is a perfect example of the correct way to handle a public misunderstanding.

If you are prepared, you can look at being confronted by the media in a much different perspective. You can consider using the media to your advantage in the event of a crisis. By working with the media, you can tell the public exactly what the facts are, what they need to know, and the details that may help you in a mission to calm parents, students, staff, and the community. Consider that it is better the media comes to you rather than taking statements from someone who does not know the whole story or has only secondhand information. If these are the people the media is forced to contact, they will most likely get false information — information that has been taken out of context or information that is misleading.

CASE STUDY: WORD FROM THE EXPERTS

Dealing with the Media

- "Do not always attack at the first moment you hear something negative. If you hear something negative, approach it in a positive way and be very upbeat." — **Oliver Phipps**

- "Don't speak unless spoken to. When you speak, say as little as necessary to get you through the interview. Also, if you don't know the answer, say nothing." — **Roy Miller**

- "Be transparent; never try to hide something because it will always come out that you were not truthful. Protecting your students has to be the first priority, and when in doubt about answering to the media, get guidance from someone who has been there." — **Barbara Belanger**

- "If you do not have a best foot to put forward, get someone else for the job. Remember that you represent more than yourself. Treat others as you would like to be treated. Be wary of what is said to the media — call your district communications office when in doubt." — **Pamela C. Mitchell**

- "Take your time, ask questions when you need to, avoid making promises you will be unable to keep, and smile a lot." — **Nancy Graham**

- "A first-year principal needs to recognize that public relations and the public's perception is critical to your success or failure. Be sure to get the good news out and control negative news. Remember to be sure to get the information across that you want, no matter what questions may be asked. Weigh your words carefully, and be a good communicator." — **James Gasparino**

- "Public relations are vital to the success of any change efforts, especially if the school had previously been seen in a negative light. Building programs that attract interest, and marketing these successes will eventually change public perception." — **Chet Sanders**

If the time comes that you must speak to the media in reference to a crisis, tell only the truth. Any lie you speak will catch up to you. If you do not know the answer to a question, tell the reporters you will get the answer and get back to them. Once you do find the answer, follow up and contact the media person that asked the question. It is also important to always look a reporter in the eye. If you are being recorded, do not look at the camera; stay focused on the question at hand. Do not elaborate, and do not become sidetracked. Sometimes it may seem the questions are harsh or accusatory, but it may be the shock and sensitivity you are feeling due to the crisis and not necessarily any criticism on the part of the reporter. Regardless, always answer forthrightly and as though the question has been asked on a normal basis. It is also important to speak of "the community" and to assure that the most important concern of the district is for the family, staff, and students. Barbara Belanger advises new principals to "be transparent. Never try to hide something because it will always come out that you were not truthful. Protecting your students has to be the first priority, and when in doubt about answering to the media, get guidance from someone who has been there."

In the world today, especially in the aftermath of Columbine and 9/11, it is not possible for a principal to honestly say, "Nothing will ever happen at my school." However, even with the violent incidents that have taken place in schools throughout the world over the last ten years, funding for safety precautions is practically nonexistent and minimal at best. Making a statement that there is not enough funding for security is not going to save you when a crisis takes place on your watch. You are going to be put under a microscope, scrutinized intensely, and possibly called upon to testify in court. Being prepared is your only option in hoping you will handle a situation accordingly.

Think back to when you were attending college, and then think of all you have heard from veteran principals on their experiences. There is no possible way college can prepare you for the job of principal. Your job is unique in that it requires on-the-job training — training that you cannot learn anywhere else. There is no possible way a school can truly prepare you for every scenario you will face each day as a principal. There are no clear-cut answers to the issues you will confront; therefore, while you are working, you are learning to tackle any situation, be it good or bad. As a principal, you will walk in the gray area throughout your career, never again having only black and white answers. The longer you work as a principal, the better you will become at doing your job. The better your relationships are with your school community, the better you will handle each incident as it occurs. To state it plainly: You, as a principal, will only be as good as your relationships with your school community.

The better principal you are, the better you will handle any situation, and the more help you will have in doing so. You will find your staff, students, and teachers standing behind you while you are doing damage control, if you are a good principal. If you are not a worthwhile leader, you are going to find yourself standing on one side of the line all alone, regardless of why the line was drawn. Strive to be a good principal, and take comfort in knowing you will not be alone in a time of crisis or in the aftermath of such.

Handling communications during a time of crisis is a gift that you, hopefully, will never need. However, it is good to know how to communicate during a crisis just in case such a situation does arise. If you are fortunate enough to have a crisis management team, a crisis response is something they, and you, should have in place. It is the crisis management team's job to assist in support not only during, but also after, a distressing event.

Some schools have an individual who will be the designated "speaker" in times of communication. It is wonderful if you have someone designated to do this, but having a backup is just as important. What if the crisis involves the speaker and he or she is unable to do the job of communicating with the community, parents, students, staff, and media? This is why a backup is so important.

The importance of your crisis management team having regular meetings and updates can never be overstated. Simulation crisis plans should be practiced. Procedures should be observed and performed. Roles should be reviewed and periodically discussed. Your school should have an emergency evacuation site, where your students and staff will go in case they must be evacuated. Your procedures for a crisis should be written and distributed to all members of the team, and your teachers and staff need to know the plan thoroughly. Remember to have contact numbers for each member of the team, which should include home, school, work, and cell numbers.

It would be helpful for you to have a good relationship with the reporter who will be responsible for news on your school. Perhaps nothing bad will ever happen at your educational establishment, but knowing the reporter at the local newspaper is still advisable. After making a phone call and scheduling an appointment, take a trip to meet the people of the local paper. With a copy of upcoming events in hand, go to the office and introduce yourself to the editor. Explain to him or her that you have school events you would like to submit, and if possible, you would like to meet the reporter who will be taking care of this information. Just as with your community, having a relationship with the local newspaper staff is a good move. Learn what the paper's deadline is, as this is important to know. You do not want to submit information at a late hour if you wish to have it in the paper the next day. Keep the names, phone numbers, fax numbers, and e-mail addresses of newspaper contacts on hand. Be sure to have a policy in your school designating personnel authorized to speak with the media. Many schools will already have this policy in place, so find out if your district does, and know exactly what that policy is.

Promoting your school is something that may or may not come natural to you. It is in your best interest, and your school's, to invite the reporter to the school for a walk-through. This is a relaxing way to communicate with him or her on your turf, and at the same time, give the reporter a chance to become more comfortable with the school building, grounds, and more important, the atmosphere.

Fielding's advice on public relations is to "…be proactive in getting out the good news." There are many wonderful things happening in schools all over the country every day. There are special awards, presentations, seminars, school plays, artistic donations, community volunteerism, and many other wonderful activities taking place all the time. Share these occasions with the media.

One last note of caution: "Off the record" is not necessarily a safeguard, regardless of your relationship with news people. Just because a reporter agrees you can speak "off the record," it does not mean what you say will not be reported. If you are lucky enough to know a reporter personally, and you are good friends with this person, you may speak off the record if you wish. Otherwise, it probably is not worth taking the chance. Barry Pichard advises first-year principals to "be careful of the press. What you say may not be what is printed. Always use your public relations department, if the school district has a contact, to bounce things off it before sending any items or talking about sensitive issues."

CHAPTER 6
Your Teachers

How important are your teachers?

"That's sort of like asking how important the sun, water, and food are to sustaining life," said John Fielding, principal of Idylwild Elementary School in Gainesville, Florida.

Although it may seem like common sense, with all the responsibility you hold as principal, you may at times lose sight of this simple truth: Without your teachers, there is no school.

"Teachers make it happen or not happen," Barry Pichard said. This is important for first-year principals to keep in mind. They are the ones responsible for educating the children, which is the ultimate point of the school system. Without them, you are lost as a principal.

Your Relationship with Teachers

The best way to build strong relationships with your teachers is to know them individually. Talk to each one of them every day, even if only for a moment. Learn their strengths and weaknesses, their talents and needs. With this knowledge, you will learn how to motivate them and encourage individual development.

Another way to encourage communication with your staff is to share the decision-making process. When you consult your staff in matters involving them and their classrooms, they will be more inclined to do a better job, because you are communicating that their opinions are important.

People are creatures of habit; change is often feared because it is unknown. If you make a change known before you implement it, it will be more easily accepted. Before marching into your new school and demanding that your teachers implement a list of new changes, start small. If you work on one teacher at a time, and you do it right, change will become contagious, and all your teachers will welcome the transition.

One place to consider suggesting changes is during meetings prior to teaching observations. Once you have your sit-in to monitor a teacher's methods, you should schedule the follow-up meeting with him or her as soon as possible. This eliminates stress and worry the teacher may be experiencing due to having a new principal, and all events that took place during the observation will be fresh in both your minds.

During the meeting, it is crucial the teacher feels as comfortable as possible; try to make the atmosphere informal, if you can. There should be no interruptions unless it is an emergency. This assures the teacher that he or she has your complete attention.

First, consider having the teacher convey how he or she feels the lesson went. Have the teacher express his or her view on how the lesson was accepted by the students. Self-reflection is good for personal growth, and oral self-assessment can cause one to realize important information that might otherwise be missed.

Once the teacher has finished his or her self-assessment, you may offer your own observations, candidly discuss the teacher's goals, and whether he or she feels those goals are being met. Be sure to commend the teacher and make some recommendations, if necessary. It is beneficial to ask the teacher what his or her feelings are on your suggestions, and find common ground.

Offering input, advice, and suggestions to someone for improving his or her work can create tension if done improperly. By asking the teacher to self-assess, you give him or her an opportunity to catch any possible mistakes or oversights. Discussing how the students absorbed the lesson also gives the teacher a chance to realize the possibility that the students are not responding, without you, the principal, having to point it out.

In order for your teachers to be receptive to your suggestions, you must have good communication skills. It is not so much what you say, but how you say it. Body language is also important when speaking to your teachers. If you ask the teacher to describe how the students received the lesson plan, and then gaze out the window while he or she starts to speak, the teacher will get the impression that you do not care. On the other hand, if he or she has your complete attention, and you make eye contact, looking away only to jot notes on his or her opinions, he or she is going to believe you are truly interested, and you have a genuine desire to help.

Another way to implement a change is to focus on the teachers who develop projects and put them into action with their students. Some principals make the mistake of focusing on that one teacher who balks at the mere mention of something new, and consequently, may immediately give up on implementing his or her idea. Instead of focusing on the negative teacher, think of the teachers in your school who show signs of innovation and creativity. These are the teachers who will support your vision. Ask those teachers to come up with new ideas, implement them in their classrooms, and share the results with you. Those results should become the talk of the day. The participating teachers will discuss the new changes with their colleagues, and their excitement over being involved should intrigue those who are not part of the experiment. This is your opportunity to create a buzz in the teacher's lounge. Share the news of how these teachers did something wonderful in their class, and show enthusiasm over it. Once this becomes an accepted change by a few good teachers, ask them to take turns visiting one another's classrooms to share their ideas, projects, and results. When the other teachers see the excitement these new changes create and realize it is working to the advantage of the teachers involved, they will want to jump on board.

One of the common mistakes made by principals is not focusing on their best teachers. When implementing change, if you focus on your best teachers, this will push the others to grow and develop their methods, too. Bounce new curriculum ideas or other changes off your best teachers, and seek their approval; the rest of the staff will be more inclined to accept the change as well. These are the teachers who have the respect of their peers, and they are the key to gaining acceptance from the others.

In implementing this new standard, you may run into disputes. There are veteran teachers who are used to doing things the same way year after year and have an aversion to trying anything different. They have taught the same curriculum, using the same methods and the same books for so long, that they go through the motions. Many times, they have no desire to do things differently. You might also run into resistance from the school board or superintendent. Stand your ground, and let it be known that this is your idea, your project, your goal, and your vision. The staff members who are enthusiastic about it will jump on board, and eventually, so will everyone else.

CASE STUDY: WORD FROM THE EXPERTS

How to Best Lead Your Teachers

- "Listening and observing are two very important things to do first. Each school has a unique culture and way of doing things. It is important to respect the current culture. Any changes that need to be made can be made by empowering staff and working with people's strengths to make an organization stronger."
  — Tammy Brown

- "I think that it is important for a first-year principal to 'fit into the school,' not have the school fit into your beliefs. The faculty and staff need to know that you are supportive of them, and they can trust you." **— Katherine Munn**

- "Principals win support best by listening to their teachers. Principals must first win their support by listening to opinions and ideas. Teachers must have a stake in decision making. When teachers have a stake in the decision making, it encourages buy-in." **— Tret Witherspoon**

- "Respect them. Understand their concerns. Serve them, and if they need something, get it." **— Oliver Phipps**

- "Always remember to communicate with them often, make them feel special, have high expectations, and most of all, be fair and consistent." **— Barbara Belanger**

- "Remember that teachers are individuals with lives outside of school. Before labeling a teacher as a 'bad' teacher, take time to talk about non-school issues in a non-threatening environment — during class change, parking lot, sitting near them at a school function. Ask about their family, vacation spots, hobbies, et cetera. Just get personal to get professional. From building trust, you can gain entry into their classroom or hearts without being perceived as a threat. Very important — let them know that you understand 'family first' — if someone is ill, or they need to take time off for a teacher conference or doctor's appointment for their child, support them. You will gain their loyalty big time." **— Pamela C. Mitchell**

- "Remember how it was when you were a teacher? If you were that teacher, what would you want done if you were in this situation? Sometimes reflective thinking before any off-the-cuff decisions are made is the best advice. It is also wonderful if you have an assistant principal to bounce ideas off of for another perspective." **— Barry Pichard**

- "Listen to concerns and do not feel obligated to make decisions immediately before understanding the impact on others." **— Leonard Weiss**

- "The best advice I have for dealing with teachers is to realize that the overwhelming majority care and want to do the best they can. Treat them with professionalism and respect." **— James Gasparino**

> • "Teachers really value autonomy; they need to be included in the decision-making process, especially over those areas that most affect them. Teachers thrive on teams; get them working together." — **Chet Sanders**

As a school leader, you must balance guidelines and rules every day. There are times you will need to make exceptions, and situations will arise when you will be faced with a tough decision. If you have someone in the school who is abusing a privilege, it would be a mistake to set a rule for everyone based on that one person. It is one person's lack of respect for school policy, not the whole teaching staff. Rather than set new rules based on one or two people who ignore current policies, find out who those people are and confront them on the issue. Otherwise, your actions are akin to a teacher disciplining a whole classroom of students for the misbehavior of one pupil. It is not a fair practice, and you may lose the faith of the rest of your staff.

Although being able to depend on your standout teachers is important, you must be careful not to treat them too much differently from their peers or lay the favoritism on too thickly. There is a fine line between showing your appreciation and making these teachers stand out so much that the rest of your staff becomes envious or disgruntled. This could cause tension among your teachers and strain your relationships with them.

A common problem in some schools is the improper placement of staff. You might find, for instance, that you have a teacher with exceptional skills and training in English, but that staff member is teaching history. This is a waste of talent and skills. Juggling the positions of teachers may or may not be feasible, but it is worth looking into. If a student attends college to become an English teacher, it is most likely because that student has a passion for English. When he or she finishes college and applies for a job, then is placed teaching a different subject, that new teacher will most likely grow unhappy or dissatisfied, which may affect his or her performance as an educator. When you place teachers in subject areas where they shine, they will be happier and thus more productive, which means your students will receive a better education. This is a sure bet on building a valuable team and earning their respect.

The most common advice veteran principals dispense is to treat your teachers with respect and provide them with as much latitude as possible to educate without distractions. "I tell my teachers that a fair amount of my job is trying to keep the nonsense away from them," said Fielding. "By nonsense, I mean things like politics, silly rules handed down from on high, all the extraneous things that the outside folks think would be a wonderful idea for schools."

In running interference, Fielding protects his teachers, and at the same time, gives them the freedom to do their job: teach. While he deals with the "nonsense," the teachers can continue to do what is best for the students.

Teacher Conflict

The issue of firing teachers is an inflammatory subject, but it is something you must be prepared to do. Chances are, at some point in your career, you will deal with an educator you deem it necessary to release, and you should know what to expect when that situation arises.

Take a moment to think of all the bad teachers you had throughout your school years. You might remember a few, possibly even three or four. Considering you had many teachers during your school career, this ratio is not horrible. However, one might wonder why those three or four were able to keep their jobs.

According to John Stossel's 2006 report on *20/20*, "Stupid in America," the teachers' union deserves much of the blame for unsatisfactory teachers being allowed to retain their positions, and by extension, it is also responsible for the failing of many schools. Stossel claimed in the report that instead of protecting good teachers, the teachers' union protects teachers who should be fired. This is a view that is shared by many in the realm of education.

CASE STUDY: WORD FROM THE EXPERTS

The Firing Process

First-year principals on how the process could be improved:

- "It is very difficult to remove a tenured teacher who is ineffective. This comes from the bargaining agreements and unions. We do have a process in place, but it takes a lot of time and effort. It seems there could be an easier way to remove someone." — **Tammy Brown**

- **Katherine Munn** said the states could "probably make [the process] a little easier. It really takes so much to get rid of low-performing teachers. In the schools that I have worked in, I haven't seen that many, but there are a few."

- "This process is handled fairly well in the state of Georgia. Administrators must allow teachers to improve delivery of instruction through a professional development plan (PDP). If, after a period of time, the teacher does not improve, the principal then gathers documentation for dismissal. This is the procedure for tenured teachers. The overall goal should be not to renew inadequate teachers who do not have tenure." — **Tret Witherspoon**

Advice from veteran principals on how to handle the process:

- "Make sure you have every [piece of] evidence you need, and you are convinced this person is bad for children. This is a person's livelihood. Do not try to get rid of a teacher just because you saw them sitting at the computer one time or because they disagreed with you. Be sure it is not [because of] personal issues." — **Oliver Phipps**

- "I don't have the authority to fire a teacher. However, I can recommend a 'non-renewal.' With that said, you need to work very closely with the teacher in question and keep HR abreast of the situation. It takes a lot of documentation to remove a tenured teacher." — **Roy Miller**

- "Do it as soon as you can; the longer you wait, the more difficult it is for you, the teacher, and your staff. Don't be afraid that it will take too much time because a poor teacher is poison to your organization and to the reputation of your entire staff." — **Barbara Belanger**

- "Make sure that you have all of your ducks in a row. Know the rules." — **Pamela C. Mitchell**

- "It is probably the hardest thing you have to do, but you have to ask yourself the question of whether you would want your own child in that room. If the answer is no, then you have no choice." — **Michael Miller**

- "Never settle. Avoid panic. Document, document, document. Would you want this teacher for your own child?" — **Nancy Graham**

- "Be sure to document; try to assist this person before considering firing." — **Robert Spano**

- "Follow procedures and consult with central office personnel. The actual firing of a teacher is usually a long process which requires tenacity and knowledge of the law by the administration." — **Leonard Weiss**

- "Firing teachers is a difficult process. It is best to terminate their employment when they are still on annual contract. If you are going to fire a teacher, work closely with your supervisor and Human resources office. You need to have well-developed documentation and patience." — **James Gasparino**

> • "Try to be out in classrooms as much as possible to develop an in-depth understanding of each teacher's level of effectiveness. Ineffective teachers should be trained to become effective or replaced." — **Chet Sanders**
>
> • "Document, document, document. Meet, offer suggestions, and document some more." — **John Redd**

Firing teachers can be difficult, and it is a long and costly process. There are times when the firing of a teacher can take several years. When a teacher is in limbo while waiting for a hearing on being dismissed, he or she still gets paid until there is a final determination, while waiting in what is commonly referred to as a "rubber room," but more officially termed a temporary reassignment center. There are times a teacher does not "qualify" for being fired due to the contract he or she works under. If a teacher is not convicted of an alleged crime or the allegations cannot be proven, he or she will usually be permanently assigned to the rubber room if considered too much of a danger to the students. Such teachers may stay in the rubber room for years while collecting a full salary for no work. Although it has become easier than it had been in the past to dismiss sex offenders or dangerous individuals, firing incompetent teachers is still a difficult process, especially if they are tenured. A 2008 report by the *Daily News* found that the New York City school district spent more than $65 million annually on teachers in the rubber room, which did not take into account the funds spent on hiring substitute teachers.

If you are in charge of a teacher whom you feel is detrimental to the students' well being, it is up to you to take charge of the situation. It is easier and less costly to hire good teachers and build the foundation of your school from the beginning than it is to try to fire bad teachers, but as a new principal, you will probably not have this luxury in the beginning. It is sometimes easier to attempt to help the bad teacher improve his or her skills than it is to fire the person. You can observe classroom activity and conference with the teacher. You can coach, suggest, and advise. However, there may be a time when you must deal with a teacher who does not pass muster as an educator. What then?

You, as a leader, are the only one who can determine whether a teacher is bad for your students. If you cannot find a way to improve the situation, you must be prepared to endure the long, painful process of terminating the teacher in question.

"Document, document, document" when trying to rid your school of a bad teacher, John Redd said. "Meet, offer suggestions, and document some more."

To cover yourself during this process, you must document everything under all circumstances. Anything related to your reason or reasons for trying to terminate a teacher must be documented, signed by the teacher, and placed in his or her file. Under the average contract, you have 90 days in which to gather your data and start the process.

When you consult with the teacher in question, be sure someone can corroborate your story. "Never meet with a teacher by yourself ... have another administrator in the meeting with you," Barry Pichard said.

If you have enough documentation accumulated in the teacher's file to justify an unsatisfactory evaluation, the matter then goes to a committee where the teacher can appeal. Thankfully, from that point on, the case is out of your hands and in the hands of the school's lawyers. Unfortunately, the repercussions are not. Your motives may be questioned, and your school board and superintendent may be upset with you because of the bad exposure the process can entail, both in the local media and with the teachers' union. However, if you do succeed in ridding your school of a problem teacher, the school community will shower you with gratitude.

Sometimes an underperforming teacher needs nothing more than a little praise. This may give the teacher needed encouragement to strive for more praise, and he or she will be more likely to trust your opinion. This is the perfect opportunity to start an open dialog, which is where those all-important communication skills come in handy. Begin by seeking a self-assessment from your teacher. Ask him or her to tell you about an assignment and what skills he or she is trying to emphasize. Ask how he or she learned a particular teaching method, and find common ground in a goal he or she mentions. This will then allow you to remind the teacher that you expect some progress toward these particular goals.

Another approach is to suggest that the teacher observe his or her peers. It is possible he or she may discover an appealing, intriguing new teaching method to try. You may also wish to send a struggling teacher to a professional development program. This attractive option may help your teacher in the following ways:

- Being surrounded by a quality team of teachers may encourage in the teacher a desire to be part of that team.

- Taking part in the team's conversation and witnessing its enthusiasm may increase the desire to improve his or her skills.

If after every effort, the teacher does not show any attempt to improve, and you decide it is in the best interest of the students — both current and future — to dismiss the teacher, it is your moral and legal duty to inform the teacher of your decision; then you should document, procure a signature, and file a report of inadequate performance. Unfortunately, though, even if the teacher has had a sexual affair with a student or has distributed drugs to students, it is no guarantee he or she will be terminated.

CASE STUDY: WORD FROM THE EXPERTS

Dealing with Conflict

- "In any kind of conflict, I feel it is important to listen first. Usually the concern is the last to come out when someone is upset. Identifying the issue and then addressing the issue in a calm and objective way usually works best." — **Tammy Brown**

- "One crucial factor is to not take sides. Find out the root of the problem and offer solutions. Never blame anyone for the conflict, even if it is obvious. Employees appreciate that." — **Tret Witherspoon**

- "Listen. Do not make rash judgments. If you need a day to think about it, take a day. And whatever decision you make, make it a win-win situation." — **Oliver Phipps**

- "If you are in the middle of the conflict, remember that you have two ears and one mouth; in other words, listen more than you talk. Also, there is more to gain if you admit that you have some responsibility in building the conflict. If you are trying to mediate a conflict, place yourself in the middle, give each side time to speak — one side speaking at a time — ask each what it is they want resolved, how can everyone make it happen. Go for win-win or close to win-win." — **Pamela C. Mitchell**

- "Conflict is usually caused by poor communication. Bring parties together to resolve conflict." — **Leonard Weiss**

- "The best advice for dealing with conflict is to realize that you cannot avoid it. It is our job to resolve conflict with compassion, sensitivity, and intelligence. Oftentimes, conflict can lead to growth for all involved — at least, that is what you should hope for." — **James Gasparino**

- "Make sure you hear both sides of a situation and make a decision. If you are not sure what to do, get some advice from the higher-ups." — **John Redd**

- "Always try to include all parties in the resolution process. Be straightforward." — **Chet Sanders**

When you become a principal, you will either be a leader who only has concern for yourself or a leader who has concern for others. If you are concerned with only yourself, it will catch up with you. The only way you can be assured that your back is covered is if you run your school with your students being the top priority. When it comes to cleaning house and ridding your educational establishment of a teacher, or teachers, of bad repute, you are either up to the task or you are not. The dismissal of bad

teachers is the ugliest part of a principal's job. Th
of the job is — or should be — living with the k
you are allowing students to be subjected to some
consider fit to teach them.

There are times when conflict within schools
distrust of the system, and there can be many re
sentiment. If a new principal comes into a schoo
establishment like a dictator, there will be conflic
tendent runs a district in a similar fashion, there
nal conflict. When a superintendent demands to
school is failing, there may be times the principa
the teachers, and the teachers will point to the
situation causes conflict.

There are many reasons for internal conflict, but it
forgotten that student education is always the m
you remain steadfast in this view, you will find sol
problems inside the school. Treat your teachers w
they deserve, and you will find ways to comm
vision, develop trust, and build a team of exceptio

It is imperative to have your teachers make regula
parents because this builds trust between teacher
It also controls and improves small problems tha
wise turn into larger concerns. Some teachers ma
to call parents for one reason or another, but getti
so is important and is in the best interest of your s
ny's grades are slipping, or Sylvia suddenly bec

tati
som
atte
trus
resu
pro
or t
situ

A tr
you
Cor
both
und
emp
trat
you

Dur
ing
This
Prir
one

al with her peers, a teacher should recognize that there is thing wrong. When a teacher brings a problem to a parent's ion, it demonstrates a concern for the student and earns the of the parent, and most likely Johnny or Sylvia will show a ant improvement in behavior or effort. Ignoring signs of a em may result in confrontation with angry or upset parents e development of deeper issues and a more troublesome ion with the student.

ining course on communication skills may be something night want to consider implementing for your teachers. nunication is imperative in resolving conflict — it allows parties to effectively reach a compromise or come to an standing on differing points of view. Such a course will wer them to commune effectively with parents, adminis- n, peers, and the community. Such training can only benefit school.

g an interview for this book, one principal mentioned hav- deal with consistent conflict between two staff members. s a nightmare for principals who have had this experience. pal Barry Pichard described his experience in handling ich situation:

"I called the two staff members into my office and got them focused on what we were going to discuss. Then I said, 'I am going to lunch duty now. When I come back to my office, I hope you two will have this worked out before I get back. The only way you can leave is if you settle this today. When I come back, if you are still here, we will continue to talk. If one of you is still here, then I guess we only have a one-sided issue that you cannot get over. If both of you are gone, then this issue is settled and all of us can move on.' When I came back from lunch, no one was in my office, and I had a note from both staff members saying, 'All is well.'"

There will be times when you are forced to play counselor for your staff, advising and guiding them in ways your schooling never prepared you for. You will reach the right solution if you take the time to know your staff personally, communicate properly, and strive to reach the best outcome for the school as a whole.

CHAPTER 7

Your Students

As a principal, you realize that major educational issues center on curricula, funding, and control. NCLB is critically important because of its implications on funding and education. Funding for the schools is complex, and the controversy over NCLB is due to the act giving the USDE the right to withhold funding. If a school is failing, and the USDE determines your school, district, or even your state, is not making efforts to comply, they can deny funds for your institution. Thankfully, most of school funding comes from the state and from local property taxes, but federal monies greatly alleviate that load and help provide your students with the education they deserve.

The implementation of good curricula is probably the easiest part of your job, once you get the teachers on board. Learning how to deal with so many different people, on so many different levels, from so many diverse views, can be challenging. Like your teachers, your personnel, the parents, and your superiors in administration, your students are also people. If you treat them with respect, you will get respect. If you let them know exactly what your expectations are, they will strive to meet those expectations. Even with the youngest students, the majority will follow the rules, if they know what those rules are.

There are numerous ways to let students know what the rules are, and what is expected of them. You can use newsletters, distribute student handbooks, post the rules on the school's website, or hold a school assembly. It is a good idea to also let the students and their parents know what the consequences are for inappropriate student behavior or poor choices.

Your Relationship with Students

As a new principal, it is imperative that you get into the hallways, the lunchroom, and the library to meet your students. Place names with faces, and remember them. It may take some time for you to do this, but you must make the effort. Visit one classroom a day until you have been to all of them and have learned whom your new students are. Greet them in the mornings, asking their names as you do so, and say goodbye to them when they are leaving in the afternoon. Make yourself visible and approachable to establish a relationship full of trust and comfort.

Communicating with students is the best way to build trust. Whether you converse while in the hallway or sit down and have lunch with them, make an attempt to give the students some of your time and learn more about them. Their opinions are invaluable, and they may make observations about the school, their teachers, or the curriculum that may surprise you. It is important to remember that the students deserve the same respect you give to parents, administrative staff, and teachers.

As a principal, you are going to hear many family secrets and information. You may learn a student's father is addicted to drugs or the mother is an alcoholic. You may discover a child's guardian is in prison for molestation. There are things you will learn that are of the strictest confidentiality. While keeping the student's best interest at heart, you must never betray that confidence and trust — and always maintain the privacy policy and confidentiality codes. If you find it might be in the best interest to get help for a student, be sure to speak with the parent about this decision before you take action. You may, at some point, be faced with turning a parent in to the police or children's services, but be sure when you come to this decision that you are doing so out of concern for the child's safety, not because of something you simply do not agree with on a personal level.

If you take the time to wander the hallways and stop in a class here and there, you are going to learn more than if you visit only during scheduled classroom visits. You will learn more about the teachers and their methods of teaching and disciplining, but you will also learn more about the students, their behavior, their attitudes, and their habits. You may realize, for instance, that a certain student named Charlotte seems to be in the hallways more than in the classrooms. This would deem checking into. You may well discover that Charlotte is a top student in the school, and the teachers send her on special errands because she is trustworthy and dependable. On the opposite end of the spectrum, you might find out she constantly asks for the bathroom pass to use her cell phone during school hours.

You will never completely rid your school of dilemmas. You will find solutions to some problems, but others will always exist.

Sometimes the best you can hope for is to be able to manage certain problems and solve others. A principal must be cautious of allowing certain dilemmas to become commonplace, and as a result, making him or her calloused. When a student must be tested for learning disabilities, for example, it might be routine for you, but it is an emotional experience for the student and the parent. It would not be in your best interest, the best interest of the parent, or that of the student, to be monotone, cold, dispassionate, and indifferent. If you act in this way, you are being an uncaring, unprofessional principal, who may never be a good leader.

Another approach to having students behave appropriately and strive to achieve good grades is to use praise and rewards. If you give praise when it has been earned, the student will desire more praise and will continue striving for good grades. Students who are praised in the classroom usually continue to show improvement, and their morale generally improves. However, the "praise and reward approach" has been debated somewhat because many schools have used the approach in hopes of inspiring all students to try harder, even those who are doing just enough to get by. Unfortunately, this sometimes has an adverse affect. Rewarding students who do average or less, may cause them to continue with the status quo instead of trying harder; if they receive the same rewards as the high achievers, there is no motivation for these students to do better. This also may have the effect of devaluing the efforts of more exceptional students. Therefore, if you do use this approach, it may be a good idea to incorporate different levels of rewards for different levels of achievement. The line should be drawn between teacher-to-student praise and rewards given at an assembly, for example. To have a student bring his or her grade up from a D to a C is, indeed, reason to give praise. At a school assembly, students are given certificates for being on the honor or merit roll. Should students be given a certificate for having brought their grades up? As principal, it is your job to decide the most effective way to implement this approach.

How you treat your students as a principal will influence the way they see you as an authority figure, and it will determine the level of trust and respect they will give you. Picture a first-year principal standing in the hallway, arms crossed, staring at the students as though he or she expects one to pull a grenade from his or her pocket while they go to their lockers. The students are going to assume this new principal does not trust them, and in return, they will not trust the new principal either. On the other hand, if the new principal smiles and greets them, introduces himself or herself, and asks their names, that principal is going to impress a hallway full of kids.

Some students may see this behavior as strange simply because they have not experienced a principal who makes such an effort to connect with his or her students, but more likely than not, the student body as a whole will appreciate this behavior. Meeting and greeting the students will allow you to build relationships with them, generate a positive atmosphere, create trust, and show the student body that you want to be involved in your school. All of these things make a great principal in the eyes of students.

It is also important to keep any reprimands or discussions about a student's behavior behind the closed doors of your office. Most students do not like to be corrected in front of their peers and may resent you for it. If you want students to listen to your suggestions, it is best to treat them with respect while at the same time remaining firm in your position of authority. It is also important not to argue with a student; the moment an argument has begun, it is lost. Remember that you are the adult, and you are in control. What you say goes. Treat your students like adults, but be clear that in the end, your word is law at school.

Student Discipline

When considering how to best reprimand students, always remember to keep the circumstances in mind. "Consider how you would want it handled if your own child was in the situation," John Fielding said. Following both pieces of advice will serve you well in navigating the rough waters of student discipline.

For example, assume you have two students named Johnny and Tom. Johnny has broken many rules over the past two years, and he seems to have an attitude that cannot be changed or improved. Johnny has been to the office numerous times and has been suspended before. If Johnny threatens another student, he will most likely receive the harshest punishment noted in his handbook. Given the circumstances of his past behavior, this seems entirely reasonable.

On the other hand, say that Tom, who has always followed the rules and is an honor roll student, happens to be experiencing a bad week. He has an altercation with Bobby, who is known to cause havoc every chance he gets. When Tom is called into the office, and you ask what happened, he explains that Bobby pushed him in the lunch line. Tom admits he pushed Bobby back after a personal insult was stated against his sister, and the fight then ensued. You know your students, and you are surprised that Tom reacted to Bobby's taunting because he would normally laugh it off and ignore it. You, as the great principal you are, ask Tom if everything is all right or if there is something bothering him because you know this is not like him. This is when Tom breaks down and tells you that his parents are getting a divorce. What you do at this point can make all the difference.

It has been proven that high-quality leaders know their students individually, and these same leaders know when to make exceptions due to this personal knowledge. You know that Tom, who would normally handle a situation such as the one with Bobby, is having a hard time at home. This would explain the reaction to Bobby's insult toward Tom's sister. To issue a harsh punishment in light of Tom's situation would not seem appropriate. However, you also realize that at least 100 students saw Tom's reaction to Bobby's insult. Those 100 students know the rules and expect there to be some kind of consequence. If you do not dole out a punishment, chances are it will come back to haunt you in due time. You can go easy on Tom and tell him, "Because you are normally a good student, and you are having some difficulties, I want you to make a visit to the counselor to talk to him."

By making an exception given the circumstance, you have left Tom's respect for his school and his teachers intact. You have let him know that you feel he is a good person and a good student, and although you understand he is troubled, it still does not make his actions excusable. You have given him a consequence, but one that is not the harshest punishment, because of these reasons. At the same time, by making him speak with the counselor, you are affording him the help he needs in coping with his parents' divorce. You have also thwarted any argument that Tom was not punished for his actions, possibly saving yourself future problems. This is why your wording in setting down rules and consequences must be carefully introduced. Every situation is different, just as every student is different. There is no such thing as a blanket penalty.

Students may not have the ability to decipher and deal with all situations, but they know right from wrong. It would be foolish to give them any less credit than that. Your students, in the above situation, are smart enough to realize Tom broke the rules, but they are also smart enough to know that Tom is normally a good student and should not be punished as harshly as others might have been in a similar situation. This is good judgment on your behalf and is a surefire way to keep the student body on your side. If you had suspended Tom, a large portion of the student body would have immediately formed a bad opinion of you, one that would likely include mistrust.

There will be times when you will be able to bend the rules for the best of the student in a way that does not harm the school's best interest. This is the case with the previous example. Unfortunately, there will also be times when you will not have such an easy decision. If you ask yourself what is best for the entire student body, it may sometimes require consequences you dislike having to implement for one or two students. As always, use your best judgment in every situation. Just as the problems that arise will all be different, so, too, are your students. You have a school full of individuals with varying personalities. With so many students in one building, there are bound to be conflicts; although you may not be able to solve every problem that lands in your lap, you should always be able to manage every situation in some capacity.

"Conflict, unfortunately, seems to be inevitable in this job," Fielding said. "If it is with the kids, the rule is: 'You tell me your side and the other does not interrupt, then we switch, and if the stories match, we figure out what to do to fix it and go back to work. If the stories do not match, we start over until they do.'"

By putting the rules on the table from the beginning of the meeting, John Fielding lets the students know there will be no tolerance for lies. The consequence will be sitting in the office until the truth, and only the truth, is told. This rule is a good one to implement for numerous reasons. It lets the students know that the situation can be easily resolved if they are honest, and it also assures them that their principal is willing to listen to both sides. If you have developed a level of trust with your students, it is more likely that they will be honest with you. Trust will open doors and reveal the truth faster than threats or yelling. Trust is a key ingredient in dealing with student conflict. "Of course, the best advice is to try to find ways to avoid conflict," Fielding said.

When dealing with young students, you should bear in mind they need structure and routine. If they do not have these settings in their home, however, you may have trouble convincing them to follow your rules. In time, though, they should come to realize that structure and routine mean security and dependability; this can eliminate behavioral problems. When you deal with young children because of misbehavior, make it known that it is not the child you are disappointed in or objecting to, but the inappropriate behavior.

CASE STUDY: WORD FROM THE EXPERTS

Disciplining Your Students

- "Treat them with respect. Sometimes they say, 'I do not know why I did it,' and they really do not know." — **Oliver Phipps**

- "When [a student is] corrected, also let them know you care and that you love them. Make family connections to build on the relationship. They want to know that you care, and if so, you will see them fewer times for negative behavior and more for just time to talk." — **Roy Miller**

- "Give your teachers power over what happens in their classrooms. Give them steps to follow and interventions to give before the administration gets involved. Train teachers to be good at disciplining their own students. When it is necessary for the administration to get involved, do not get angry or 'even.' State the policies and procedures, and follow through with them equally with every student." — **Barbara Belanger**

- "Dignity — do not take it away from them. No matter what the student did, he or she knows that his authority is less than yours. He knows that he has little or no power. A student and his or her parent will be more accepting of the discipline consequences and more sorrowful for and reflective of the misbehavior if the student can walk out of the school without shame." — **Pamela C. Mitchell**

- "Be sure students know the expectations, and then be sure to dole out the consequences promised. Kids do what is expected of them ... and they really want — and need — parameters in spite of their objections to the contrary." — **Nancy Graham**

- "Students must understand that the classroom is not a place to disrupt. Very simply stated, 'Teachers have a right to teach, and students have a right to learn.'" — **Robert Spano**

- "Being fair when disciplining a student does not always mean treating everyone the same. If it is a minor incident, deal with it, and get them back to class. Usually, these are the students who can least afford to miss instruction. Inform parents when appropriate. Do not let anyone intimidate others. No one should be afraid to be in school. Follow district guidelines and consult with your supervisor when in doubt." — **James Gasparino**

- "Schools should try to change negative behavior through progressive disciplinary actions. A representative group should develop a school-wide plan. All staff and students should be trained." — **Chet Sanders**

- "Question everyone you can before making a decision. Do not be as rough on them the first time. If they mess up again, stiffer punishment [is required]." — **John Redd**

If you have a staff that shows mutual respect for one another as well as to the rest of the personnel and the students, discipline problems should already be greatly reduced.

This will hold true for schools that house all ages. Setting rules and explaining them to the students will also help eliminate discipline problems. When you show that every person in your school is valued as an individual, you pave the way for an atmosphere that is inviting, cheerful, successful, and orderly. This also affords students a sense of pride in their school and fosters acceptance of rules and expectations. This will allow you to stop many potential problems before they occur.

If you have a policy in place defining your expectations on how problems are to be dealt with, then fewer problems will end up at your door. Have this policy listed in the student handbook, newsletters, and announcements. Finding solutions to conflict and concerns should start on the level where the problem exists, and if no solution agreed on, it should then be taken to the next level. When parents have complaints and concerns they wish to bring to the school's attention, the hierarchy should be in this order:

- Go first to the teacher or head of the subject department.

- If the matter cannot be resolved at this level, then go to the principal.

- If you cannot solve the problem, the parent should then go to the superintendent.

- The final level would be the school board.

The procedure for student discipline should be handled a little differently. First, make sure all teachers have their own disciplinary guidelines outlined in their classrooms. A good example of steps to follow is:

1. **Give a reminder first**. This can be done for one or two students, or for the whole class. Giving a reminder is also giving the benefit of the doubt. By doing this, the teacher is letting the student(s) or the class know that he or she realizes they may have forgotten the rules and can then remind them of the policy in place. This is also a way to — and the time to — stop the problem before it escalates.

2. **Give a warning.** By warning the student(s) or class, the teacher is now giving a reprimand. A warning for a student should not be said across the room, but instead directly between teacher and student.

3. **Give a written warning**. The written warning should have the offensive behavior printed out and should be sent home with the student to be signed by parents. If the student does not return the paper, he or she will be sent to the office. At this time, the teacher should remind the student of the next step in disciplinary action.

If the issue extends beyond the written warning, the teacher then needs to bring the matter to you. If the issue at hand involves a conflict between two students, the following guidelines should be followed to resolve this conflict:

- Schedule a face-to-face meeting with the teacher and students.
- All students involved in the conflict will meet with the teacher.
- Students will follow the advice of the teacher to resolve the conflict.
- Students will make an agreement with the teacher on behavior.
- The teacher will contact the parents.
- As a last resort, the students will be sent to your office.

Placing these procedural expectations in your handbook(s), as well as in newsletters, announcements, and on the school website should eliminate the amount of complaints you field. It will also show that you have trust in your teachers to handle any problems that may arise. You should never take it for granted that your policies are being followed. Always check with your teachers to be sure parents are informed, students are taken care of correctly, and conflicts are managed properly.

Many principals advise a "cooling down" period for students before you try to talk to them about a given problem. Especially when dealing with a fight or an argument, allowing a student time to calm down is extremely important. Barry Pichard said it is wise to "make sure you have the entire story before proceeding with any discipline."

"Discipline is probably one of the hardest things to do because you have the final word on whether a student stays in school, is suspended, or expelled," he said. "Discipline, or should I say good discipline, involves counseling and time. The time spent with a student or group of students may limit the time you have to spend with them in the future about the same issue or situation."

Taking the time to know your students as individuals and being aware of the circumstances will always guide you to the right solution.

"When you think you have the entire story, you look at the puzzle and see what the picture really looks like," Pichard said. "Sometimes it comes together quite nicely, and it is clear and concise. Other times it looks like some old puzzle that has a few pieces missing, and you will never find them. ... Discipline [is] probably the most time-consuming and worst aspect of the job."

Take every aspect of each individual situation into account whenever doling out punishment, and go with your gut feeling whenever some of those puzzle pieces are missing.

Bullying

One aspect of student discipline that has become increasingly important for principals to be aware of is recognizing the signs of bullying. Recent research and studies have shown that the most serious, violent incidents in schools are a direct result of bullying, including school shootings and suicides. But these instances only represent a fraction of the widespread problem. According to a 2001 survey by the National Institute of Child Health and Human Development, more than 16 percent of U.S. students reported being the victims of bullying at the time of the survey.

A study from the same survey, published online at the *Journal of Adolescent Health* website (**www.jahonline.org**) showed that students who identify as gay or lesbian are more likely to be the victims of bullying. Gay males had double the risk of experiencing bullying, while homosexual females were three times as likely to be bullied.

With the emergence of social media, such as Facebook®, Twitter®, and MySpace®, and technological advances, such as text messaging and chat, bullies have found a new outlet for their taunting. Cyberbullying extends the instances of torment from beyond the classroom to the home, where bullies can now taunt and insult behind screens. Though much of this breed of bullying is done at home, that does not mean it is out of your realm of responsibility; just like regular bullying, the effects can and will still be felt at school.

In the News: Use Caution in Cyberbullying Cases

Although it is important to monitor your students' online activity for instances of cyberbullying, you must consider the situation carefully before taking serious steps to solve a potential problem. One cautionary tale comes from Florida, where a University of Florida student sued her former high school over punishment for what the principal saw as the cyberbullying of a teacher.

The student, Katherine Evans, was suspended from Pembroke Pines Charter High School in 2007 for creating a Facebook page on her home computer titled, "Ms. Sarah Phelps is the worst teacher I've ever met." She invited current and former students of Phelps to post their own criticisms. Some did, while others posted in defense of the teacher and criticized Evans for creating the page. Evans took down the Facebook page after a few days; according to court documents, Phelps never saw the page.

According to a February 2010 article in the *New York Times*, Evans was suspended two months later. A CNN.com article stated the principal at the time suspended her for three days for disruptive behavior and cyberbullying a staff member, and she was also removed from Advanced Placement classes and placed in regular classes instead.

With the lawsuit, Evans sought to remove the suspension from her disciplinary record and have it rendered invalid; she also sought a nominal amount in damages for the violation of her First Amendment rights and to cover her legal fees, her lawyers said.

The former principal, Peter Bayer, had asked that the case be dismissed. But Magistrate Judge Barry L. Garber rejected the motion and ruled that Evans' criticism of her teacher was a First Amendment matter.

"Evans' speech falls under the wide umbrella of protected speech," Garber wrote in his order. "It was an opinion of a student about a teacher, that was published off-campus … was not lewd, vulgar, threatening, or advocating illegal or dangerous behavior."

The judge's ruling serves as an appropriate measuring stick when dealing with a potential instance of cyberbullying. It is important to distinguish between opinion or criticism and threatening or vulgar comments.

"It used to be that principals would not hear you talking about teachers outside the class," said Ryan Calo, an attorney with Stanford Law School's Center for Internet and Society. "Social networks give principals the ability to see what students are saying about teachers and each other. It is one thing to use that information to identify illegal or dangerous conduct. It is quite another to punish opinion and speech outside the classroom that does not disrupt the activities of the classroom," he told CNN.

The serious, violent cases only show the consequences of bullying that pushed its victims beyond their breaking points. Research has established a link between childhood bullying and increased mental and physical health problems in adulthood. A January 2010 study published in the *Australian and New Zealand Journal of Psychiatry* found that adults who suffered from bullying as children were more likely than others to suffer from depression and anxiety, fatigue, and pain, among other physical effects.

This research has led to an increase in responsibility for school administration in bullying prevention. It is imperative not only to recognize the signs of bullying and put a stop to it before the torment results in a homicide or suicide, but also to work to thwart bullying before it even begins. This is an important part of keeping your school safe for all students.

As principal, you must first ensure that you, your faculty, and your staff know how to recognize the signs of a potential bullying problem. Bullying, as defined, is not an isolated incident, but rather a pattern of behavior repeated against an individual, or individuals, over a period of time. It can be either physical or mental — or both. Bullying behaviors include:

- Verbal abuse and harassment, including that of a racial or sexual nature

- Physical abuse and harassment

- Visual abuse, such as making obscene gestures to another person

- Threatening harm to an individual and/or the individual's family

- Deliberate exclusion of an individual from a peer group

- Spreading false rumors about another individual

- Sending demeaning or threatening notes or e-mails

- Making demeaning or threatening phone calls

- Stealing or destroying another individual's property

- Playing pranks on another person in front of a peer group

- Drawing obscene or humiliating graffiti about another person

- Stalking another person to incite fear

There are many types of bullies, just as there are various ways to bully a victim. However, you should know some common bully characteristics. Bullies usually:

- Like to dominate others

- Use others to get what they want

- Have trouble seeing a situation from another person's point of view

- See their feelings and needs as more important than those of others

- Hurt other children when adults are not present

- Use blame and false allegations to project their own low self-worth onto their victims

- Will not accept responsibility for their own actions

- Cannot foresee the consequences of those actions

- Crave attention

- Feel contempt toward their victims

Although it is impossible for school administrators to be everywhere at all times in order to monitor any type of bullying behavior, it is crucial that your school employs an anti-bullying system. There may already be anti-bullying measures in place at your school. However, if there are not, there are some steps you can take to better arm yourself and your staff in facing this widespread problem. The key when establishing an anti-bullying policy is to also cultivate a welcoming environment at your school where children feel comfortable sharing with their teachers. Kids need to know not only that bullying is wrong, but also that if they are the victims of bullying or witness another student bullying someone else, the teachers are trustworthy and there to listen and help.

In his 1993 book *Bullying in School*, Dan Olweus identified numerous ways schools can become more proactive about bullying. Olweus suggested that teachers and administrators closely monitor lunches, recess, and outdoor activities for any harmful behaviors. It is also important that teachers and parents are unified on the issue and maintain open communications concerning any possible instances of bullying. Assemblies, workshops, and parent/teacher conferences geared toward bullying issues can be helpful. You may also want to consider setting up a contact phone number that victims can call if they want to report what is happening to them, but fear retaliation if the bullies find out they told an administrator. This way, you at least are made aware of the situation and can counsel with your teachers and guidance counselors about a school-wide measure to eradicate the problem.

Here are several more steps you can take to establish a zero-tolerance environment for bullying at your school, as outlined by George Varnava in his 2002 book *How to Stop Bullying in Your School*:

1. Formulate a whole-school action plan with all sectors of the school community represented in the plan.

2. Establish a commitment: "We aim to be a bullying-free school."

3. Publicize the commitment internally and externally, providing a basis for collaboration with parents and the local community.

4. Introduce a practical anti-bullying program in the school.

5. Self-audit to determine if your program is working.

6. Take action to address specific risk areas.

7. Undertake a whole-school review of the anti-bullying process.

8. Formulate criteria for evaluating your progress and reducing bullying.

Above all, remember that in order to really know what is going on in your school, you must ask the children. It is suggested that you implement an anonymous survey to ascertain the level of bullying present in your school. When determining how to discipline bullies, keep in mind that escalated bullying should carry severe consequences, whereas a student expressing a genuine desire to change should be applauded.

For more resources on bullying and bullying prevention, visit the International Bullying Prevention Association's website at **www.stopbullyingworld.org** or see Atlantic Publishing Group's *The Complete Guide to Understanding, Controlling, & Stopping Bullies & Bullying: A Complete Guide for Teachers and Parents* by Margaret R. Kohut.

CHAPTER 8

The Parents

"Parents have changed dramatically in the last five years," Barry Pichard said. "Before, I would have some students who were rude and disrespectful to teachers and school staff, but now the students are taking their cue from their best teachers, their parents, because they see them being rude and disrespectful to school staff when they are at conferences and meetings."

This makes a statement not only about how a principal must deal with rude and disrespectful parents, but also about how this change in society has had a trickle-down effect, altering the way each generation views, and subsequently treats, authority figures and peers.

What are the teachers and principals expected to know, teach, and supply now that they were not before? Compared to as many as 20 years ago, many changes have taken place in society, which means the schools have had to change, too. In the past, a principal seldom had to worry about the heightened controversy or concern over such subjects as:

- Sex education and condoms
- The teaching of creationism along with evolution
- Free breakfast and free lunches for students whose family income falls into poverty level
- Inclusion for students with disabilities
- Students being excused from the Pledge of Allegiance for religious reasons
- The No Child Left Behind Act, literacy, and standardized tests
- Same-sex marriage and gay rights issues
- Latchkey kids
- School safety and preventing school violence
- Increased funding issues
- Inequality and racism
- English as a second language
- Sexual harassment, molestation, or rape of students

Today's great principals view parents as partners, and most educational establishments benefit from this perspective when it is put into practice. Many times parent-teacher organizations and/or associations provide funding for necessities, such as classroom or playground equipment. Parents can be a tremendous asset, or they can be like a painful thorn on what might have once appeared to be a beautiful rose.

Your Relationship with Parents

For the most part, parents want and expect the same things from you as their children do. The following is a list of some expectations parents have:

- Be fair.
- Be caring.
- Be consistent.
- Keep them informed.
- Keep their child safe.
- Show respect.
- Work with them.
- Make sure your faculty is teaching their children what they need to know.
- Make school an enjoyable experience for their children.

Parents expect to be informed of where their tax money is going, but some administrators are perturbed by what they perceive as interference. Principals would be wise to treat all parents with respect for the following reasons:

- The tax dollars of the parents' hard-earned money provides for much of your paycheck as well as the education of your students.

- Parents volunteer for many events, relieving principals and teachers from longer hours.

- Parent involvement can help boost morale for everyone in the school.

- Parents can be your biggest fans and strongest allies.

- Word-of-mouth communication between parents travels faster than any other form of communication and is good for public relations.

- Parents can save your job by letting the school board know they support you.

- Studies have shown that involved parents produce excellent students.

- Involved parents support school programs monetarily, by attending events and by encouraging their children to be involved.

- Positive relationships with parents influence relationships with students.

By expressing an interest in the lives of students and their families, you can make all the difference in how parents support the school district — and the parents are the ones who vote. On the other hand, principals must draw the line with family involvement the same as they must do with teachers and their personal problems. It is not wise to get involved in the personal problems of families any more than necessary. When a problem interferes with the student's behavior, schoolwork, or relationships with peers, you have a responsibility to help that student as much as possible. Beyond that, it is wise to stay out of the mix. However, parents will be assured when dealing with personal crises that their children are in the hands of a principal they admire and respect.

It is also important to understand that students who have involved parents are more successful in school. There have been many studies done to show the difference in students with involved parents and those without, such as the American Education Research Association study titled "1997 Review of Educational

Research." Parental involvement is important for your students and for you because when parents are left out of the loop, distrust and hard feelings can occur. The research shows:

- The earlier in a child's education the parents become involved, the more powerful the effect.

- The most effective form of parent involvement takes place when parents work directly with children on learning activities at home.

- 86 percent of the public believes that support from parents is the most important way to improve the schools.

- The biggest problem facing the schools is lack of parental involvement.

- Decades of research shows that parent involvement gives students:
  1. Higher test scores, graduation rates, and grades
  2. Better school attendance
  3. Increased motivation and better self-esteem
  4. Lower rates of suspension
  5. Decreased use of drugs and alcohol
  6. Fewer incidences of violent behavior

- Parent involvement in education is twice as predictive of student academic success as family socioeconomic status.

- The more intense parent involvement is, the more successful the achievement.

Regardless of whether your students are exceptional, average, or have problem areas, it is beneficial to all of your students to have parental involvement, and, therefore, it is beneficial to you as an effective principal.

Developing good relationships with parents involves communication. Usually, parents and guardians learn about the principal through newsletters or other forms of communication from the school. If they come to an open house or teacher-parent conferences, they might meet you for a minute or two and get nothing more than a first impression — although first impressions can leave lasting impressions. It is in your best interest to meet as many parents or guardians as possible at such gatherings. Most parents desire opportunities to communicate with the principal just as they do with teachers.

If meeting with a parent over an incident involving his or her child, it would be wise to start the conversation by pointing out the good qualities of the student, and then dive into the bad news as gently as possible. After all, you and the parents have the student's best interest at heart. It is important to treat all parents with respect, and use your best judgment in determining how to discipline a student to avoid angering a parent. Unfortunately, in some circumstances, this may be unavoidable despite your best efforts.

You may find that some parents had problems with the previous principal. If, by chance, the parent comments on past problems, do not ignore his or her statements, but instead acknowledge them. These are problems or issues that you have inherited, and only you can correct them. Let the parent know you were not aware, or you were aware, of the problem, and it is an issue you have every intention of resolving. It is also possible these parents simply want to be involved, but have been turned away in the past. Attempt to find a place they can be drawn in, and you may be surprised at how quickly their attitude will turn around.

If you treat everyone as though they are good, they most likely will be. This is true with all people you will have contact with as a principal. Teachers, students, and parents want to be treated well, and who can blame them? Suppose, for instance, you have a problem student named Johnny. You have learned through staff members and other students that Johnny's parents are divorced, he lives in poverty, and he has a terrible attitude due to an uninvolved father. If you treat Johnny's mom as though she is a worthless parent, she will have no reason to want to act any different. However, if you treat her with respect and find good qualities in Johnny to discuss with her, perhaps she will strive to improve her parenting skills, simply because she enjoyed being shown some respect.

Communication, respect, and a good attitude are the three fundamentals in maintaining good standing with parents. Make all communication as positive as possible. In his book, Todd Whitaker suggested that by focusing on bad teachers or bad parents when communicating with a group or an individual, you are making good people feel uncomfortable. Instead of generalizing and including good parents in this announcement or speech, find a way to single out that belligerent parent, relieving the good parents from being included in a group in which they do not belong.

"If applied consistently … who is most comfortable, and who is least comfortable…it can bring simplicity to your decision on your approach," Whitaker said. "It is never the good parents or the good teachers that you want to make uncomfortable."

Some conflicts may put you in the middle of an angry parent and a teacher. Even if you agree with the parent's complaint, it is in your best interest to back the teacher as a member of your staff. However, you need to assure the parent that you are sorry this misunderstanding has occurred and that the issue will be discussed with the teacher. With this approach, you are not necessarily taking sides, but you will assure the parent and stand behind your teacher at the same time. If you do not back your teacher, he or she may lose trust in you, and this could have a domino effect with your staff.

However, if you have doubts that the teacher's behavior or choice was correct, it would be advisable to let the parent know that you will examine the situation thoroughly — and then follow through with that promise. Otherwise, you may come across as indifferent or uncaring, and it may seem to the parents as if you were just dismissing them when you agreed to do so. If a parent takes the time to contact you, it is because that parent is concerned about his or her child. A parent's concern over a child's welfare should never be treated indifferently. After all, that child is one of your students, and his or her well being is supposed to be your first priority.

One of the hardest things to deal with as a principal is receiving complaint after complaint from parents about a certain teacher. Concerned parents may come to your office demanding to know why nothing is being done about that horrible history teacher; they will not want to hear that firing a teacher is difficult because of the drain on time and money the process usually entails. Most parents assume you have full control over the situation, when that is not the case.

Recall Mr. Waltin from Chapter 2, the teacher with an inability to deal with students and his own anger management issues. The school principal listened to many parental complaints about this teacher, but when the issue evolved into a physical threat to a student, as a leader he was forced to do something. The principal took the issue to the superintendent, and as a result, the teacher was removed from a teaching position and put into a low administrative position. The most important aspect of this decision is that the teacher was removed from having contact with students. An unrelated positive was that because the teacher was not dismissed, the district saved money.

In an incident such as this, you will usually have to deal with some fallout. Parents will want to know why the problem was not resolved before physical contact with a student became an issue. Some parents will question if the principal should have done something earlier. Some parents might blame the principal for allowing the problem to exist for so long. Parents will wonder how many students suffered because of, or were affected by, this teacher not being dismissed earlier.

In an establishment where there are so many varying personalities, there will always be some conflict. It is important to realize that as a principal, you are the symbolic figurehead of the school. Your presence is expected at many events, and you are the spokesperson for the staff, students, and sometimes the district. As principal, you will interact with many people, and how you treat them and assist in resolving their conflicts will make or break your reputation.

Just as you should instruct your teachers to contact the parents of a child when an issue arises concerning the student, you should also do the same if a problem is brought to your attention. It is your responsibility to make sure contact is made, and the parents are informed of the issue. This will help prevent conflict down the road. Like teachers, parents want to be informed. When they are not informed, bad situations can arise. When parents are left out of the loop in matters concerning their children, they tend to get angry. After all, their children are supposed to be the focus of the schools — and you, as principal. It is up to you to make sure they are all right.

Some schools create a parent handbook as well as a handbook for the staff and the students. Handbooks could be beneficial and may help eliminate some problems before they have a chance to occur. Another way to do this is to ensure the parents are informed of how their students are doing. Keep parents up to date on:

- Student grades
- Student progress, or lack thereof
- School policies, new or changed
- School board meetings
- Long-term substitute teachers
- Assemblies

- School calendars

- Special curricula

- Standardized test scores

- Student behavior

- Changes in curricula

Parents and guardians generally want to be kept apprised of their children's progress. In order to do this more effectively, some schools in the country have instituted an online grading system that parents may access. The programs provide access to student assignments as well as posted grades for tests, quizzes, homework, and papers. This is very effective for parents who want to know what is going on with their children. They can access the information on a regular basis from their own computers at their convenience and at any time of day or night. These programs also offer the ability to click on an e-mail link to contact the teacher with questions and concerns. One such commonly used application is called eSchoolBook (**www.eschoolbook.com**). The program is set up by the school district and is maintained by the technology department. Teachers are expected to enter grades on a weekly basis unless otherwise specified, although parents and students can access them daily to see any updates.

The eSchoolBook information is password-protected, so no one else can access the information. Currently, the district provides the information online for grades six through 12. Additionally, family members are linked, so parents can access all their children with one password. The school district requires parents to attend a seminar explaining the program. Subsequently, they must fill out an application and produce their driver's licenses to prove who they are. The application is reviewed before it is submitted to the technology department, which adds an element of safety. If your district does not employ such a program, you may wish to see if this is possible.

Some schools run their establishments with the concept that parents are important partners. Some schools provide parents with lists of people to contact with specific complaints or concerns, which can easily be found on the school's website and in newsletters that are sent home. Using a chain of command for concerns and complaints will help eliminate drains on your precious time and possible escalations of conflict. If a parent has a disagreement with a teacher, for example, and he or she bypasses that teacher, such action tends to make the situation worse. Set a rule that parents with complaints or concerns should attempt to solve the problem by taking it to the appropriate level first, then following up by taking it to you only if necessary.

Parents are the same as teachers when it comes to following your expectations. They will abide by your rules if you make them clear and explain your reasons for the rules. By doing so, you are showing them respect and at the same time asserting your authority as principal.

CHAPTER 9
Focusing On You

You are going to experience many changes in your life once you become a principal. You may have experienced some of these already, but there are more to come. The need to do your job and do it well may cause you to become fixated, and you may lose sight of your personal life, as well as what it was before you were a principal. In order to mesh the two, your previous life and your life now, it will take work, patience, management, and plenty of courage. This book is designed to help you do this.

How Important are You?

According to the Southern Regional Education Board (SREB), you are extremely important. SREB, an Atlanta-based policy group whose mission is to help its member states achieve the 12 Challenge to Lead Goals for Education, concludes that there are many prospective principals with the proper educational credentials, but few who are capable of being good school leaders. The shortage of these potential leaders is "crucial," according to SREB.

The group states the role of principals in improving schools and increasing student achievement is also crucial. They have identified 13 critical success factors that are associated with principals who have improved student achievement in their schools. These factors are:

- Focusing on student achievement

- Developing a culture of high expectations

- Designing a standards-based instructional system

- Creating a caring environment

- Implementing data-based improvement

- Communicating

- Involving parents

- Initiating and managing change

- Providing professional development

- Innovating

- Maximizing resources

- Building external support

- Staying abreast of effective practices

Also, according to SREB, when considering the characteristics of a good school principal, one must look for the following:

- One who can make constructive and beneficial decisions for students, staff, teachers, parents, community, and the establishment as a whole

- One with motivation and determination

- One who has good leadership and supervisory skills

- One who can communicate effectively

- One with knowledge in educational practices

- One who is computer savvy

The principal is responsible for setting the atmosphere for the entire school. If you are a strong leader, you will be followed. On the opposite end of the spectrum, a bad principal can ruin a good school in as little as a few weeks. Bringing around a troubled and failing school may take more time, but a good principal can certainly achieve that attainable and worthwhile goal. Good principals are a draw for good teachers. Bad principals chase away good teachers.

A good principal needs to know how students learn and how teachers teach. In knowing these two important elements, you are already halfway to the goal of becoming a good leader. This knowledge will help you when choosing new curricula and resources for your teachers. However, you must also understand the necessity of caring about the individual students, staff, and the school community as a whole.

If you understand how students are currently learning, and how your students learn best, you already have a deep understanding of your student body. If you understand that your teachers need to constantly improve their own skills, you already have set a goal for them to meet, a goal that will help your students, staff, and school community become successful.

Basically, it all comes down to you. When things go well for your school community, it will most likely be the school board and the superintendent who get the credit. When things go bad, you will get the blame. You are responsible for what happens in your school, the outcome of your students' education, whether or not you have good or bad teachers, how well or poorly they teach, and the success or failure of your students as future citizens. In looking over this partial list, it is easy to see why you are crucially important as a principal.

Although you will take the fall alone if there is a catastrophe or incident in your school, you need a team to accomplish your goals. When asked, good principals admit they are responsible for their school and all who attend it, but if their school is recognized as an excellent school, or one that has been turned around, they will be the first to tell you that they did not do it alone. When great principals work with a team of teachers from their schools, they are also helping to groom leaders for the future. Imagine going to a meeting or seminar with a group of teachers. What will happen after the meeting, during the ride home? You will converse with one another about the speaker and toss around ideas. This will aid in creating a unified vision, fostering relationships, delegating responsibility, and training your teachers to become future school leaders.

For some people, giving up power is not easy. As a good principal who wishes to have a good team, you will need to give up some of your authority. Delegating responsibility means allowing someone else to be in charge of a certain criteria. You are still responsible, but if you are wise, you will share that responsibility and give yourself a break while giving someone else a chance to lead in an area where they fit best.

As a dedicated leader, you are the one the school community will turn to. You are the one who makes the decisions; implements the changes; encourages and listens to others; assembles meetings; improves the school in every regard; and rewards the teachers, staff, and students. You are expected to stand beside your staff and students when they need you. To be a leader, you must influence the goals of others and motivate them to achieve these goals. You are the one who holds everything together in your school.

Some states are looking at a crucial shortage of good leadership applicants. A 2003 Michigan State University study found that Michigan schools had half as many applicants for principal positions than there had been in 1988. Florida was similarly in a crucial state of affairs with a majority of its principals about to retire. With the blessing of the states, the school districts made an offer to their principals and were relieved to have the majority agree to stay in order to work with candidates who wished to become principals.

Exactly what makes a qualified principal? According to a personnel director in Michigan quoted in the aforementioned study, it takes seven years to become a competent teacher, and the candidates they had applying for principal positions had only three years of teaching under their belts. With the large number of retiring principals looming ahead coupled with the shortage of qualified candidates, some states are extremely concerned about what will happen to their schools in the future. Fewer applicants can be explained in that the role of principal is less desirable due to the additional burdens a principal must carry. The problem of less qualified applicants is a mystery, however. Some believe that teachers are more satisfied in their positions today than before, due to better pay and retirement plans and more resources. Still, good principals are harder to come by, which means students will have a harder time learning in quality schools.

There have been articles written in which principals are compared to Wonder Woman or Superman. With the endless jobs you are required to perform, it is no surprise. Many communities are aware of how the position of school leader has changed and are now hiring assistant principals or administrative assistants. Those job descriptions, however, may depend on the principal's own preference. Principals, like teachers, are individuals, and the responsibilities they are willing to delegate to someone else would depend on that principal as an individual. One principal may be good at public relations while another is better at choosing and placing curricula.

When asked which responsibility they enjoy most, the majority of the principals interviewed for this book gave a surprising answer: student discipline. It seems the greatest leaders enjoy the direct contact with their students and helping steer them toward good choices. Giving reinforcement and being a patient guide for students to become good citizens is most important to good leaders. Many principals also said that spending time with their students, even in the matter of discipline, is how they know what is really happening in their school. One principal said he has a way of talking to students when they are in trouble so that they want to do better, and he takes the time to check on them periodically afterward, so they know he cares.

The three duties principals enjoy the least are dealing with are upset parents, budgeting, and teacher evaluations. Budgeting is very time-consuming, evaluations never seem to work in improving teaching habits, and parental complaints are the greatest annoyance principals must deal with on a regular basis.

In today's society, the schools are always being second-guessed. Schools have been put in a position where they must be on the defensive. There are greater demands on your time, more complex social issues to navigate, more numerous responsibilities to attend to, and therefore, more stress in your job description. These issues and more are reasons there are fewer qualified candidates looking to become principals. Yet, here you are, a first-year principal about to embark on a ride you will never forget.

This is why you, as a first-year principal, must take into consideration yourself as a person, not just as a principal.

"As a principal your work is never done, but you have to make the decision that enough is enough, and that sometimes you need time for yourself … I know this is a problem for, especially, new principals."

Barbara Belanger, principal
Harbor City Elementary School
Melbourne, Florida

Taking Care of You

Since the traditional expectations of principals remain and even more have been added to the list, there is a great concern of burnout for school leaders. With 12- to 15-hour days being common, night activities you must attend, meetings you must schedule, state mandates you must follow to the letter, teacher evaluations to be done, researching and implementing of resources, attending seminars, meeting with parents, and disciplining students, many would ask why anyone would want to be a principal. Still, there are those of you who do. In order to be successful, you must remember one important ingredient in the mix: taking care of yourself.

If you do not take care of yourself, how are you going to take care of all those students who depend on you to be there for them?

You were most likely a teacher before you became a principal. If this is the case, you now find yourself on a different playing field than where you once were. You are no longer a teacher, and you will not be treated as one of the group. It is not so much that you are no longer liked or appreciated; it is more that you are no longer one of them. You are now an administrative figure, the authoritarian, and above all, you are the one who can have them fired.

At first, you may feel isolated in your new role. Leaders are not one of the gang, but rather an entity all on their own. You do not belong with the superintendent, or the teachers, so where do you belong? It is advisable that you find other principals you can talk to. Numerous states now have mentorship programs for principals. Check to see if your state offers one. Some states make it mandatory for first-year principals to attend these programs before becoming a principal. They are an invaluable resource.

Not only might you experience loneliness upon assuming your new role, but also you may feel sadness. You are giving up a position you knew and were comfortable with. Now you have taken on something that is much bigger than you are used to, and you may, at first, be uncomfortable as an authority figure. This is to be expected, so take heart. It is perfectly normal for those who make a life change and leave something familiar behind to feel nostalgic for a while. It is much like leaving a part of yourself behind.

You may take the position as principal at the school where you taught. You will probably expect everything to remain the same, but some principals who have done this have said it was not a good move. Though they were still surrounded by the same teachers with whom they once shared camaraderie, some of their colleagues shunned the new principals. Such behavior could be due to jealousy, envy, a sense of betrayal or distrust, or possibly even anger. It is also possible some of the teachers will attempt to take advantage of your past friendship and new position by coming to you with complaints and expecting favorable action. There may come a time when you enter the teacher's lounge and all conversation stops. This kind of reaction will hurt your feelings and make you feel awkward, lonely, and isolated. Take comfort in the knowledge that, in time, things will grow to be somewhat normal once your teachers become accustomed to your leadership. However, you should not expect to ever be "one of the gang" again. You are now the commanding officer, not one of the brigade members.

You must take time for your family and friends, and for yourself, and you will find this is not so easy to do. On the typical day, you rose from bed with the alarm at 5:30 a.m. and arrived at work by 6:45 a.m. You have been on the move all day, and finally, the dismissal bell rings. You stand at the door and say goodbye to the students and teachers, then go to your office to take care of some paperwork. You enter your room to find the pile of papers has somehow grown, and the small stack has quadrupled in size. There are also small Post-it® notes with messages the secretary left, callers who wish to speak with you, the small yellow squares having taken over your desk while you were out. You take a deep breath and start going through the mound of papers, placing them in order according to priority. With that pile now in order, you go through the yellow sticky notes, placing them in a line, most important first. You hear the last bus pull out of the parking lot and start making the phone calls, knowing that to answer to all of them will take at least two hours. That still leaves the pile of paperwork you must finish, and the length of the night ahead stretches in front of you.

Some people have a tendency to refuse to quit until the job is finished. This can be a wonderful quality or a horrid curse. As a principal, you must constantly remind yourself that your job is truly never done. You must force yourself to know where to draw the line, put aside your remaining work, and pack it in for the night. If you do not follow this rule, you will never see your family. If you let the job completely take over your life, you will burn out within three years and never be the wonderful leader you have the potential to become.

You may find that your role in friendships also changes. You may feel like you are the same person, but you will not be viewed the same by others. You may find some friends simply disappear or do not return your calls. It is not easy to understand, but there are those who may feel you are on a different level with your new position and are thus uncomfortable with this change.

Your family may have thought they knew what to expect with your new role as principal, but you may find your spouse becomes upset that you are not getting home until 8 p.m., rather than the usual 4 p.m. Rather than become estranged from your family, force yourself to designate a stopping point, and go home once you reach it. No, you may not get all your paperwork finished or return all your calls, but you will have some time with your family, and that is the priority you must keep in mind. There will always be paperwork to do and calls to return, but your children will not be young forever, and your spouse may grow weary of effectively becoming a single parent.

There is support out there for first-year principals. Your secretary may become your confidante, or it may be one of the teachers, or even the custodian. Regardless, you will find the one person you can confide in, relate your troubles to, or simply vent frustrations to. Whoever this person is, he or she will always be there, taking the time to listen and never saying a word to the rest of the staff in regard to your troubles and worries. A principal in another school may capture your friendship, but most likely, there will be at least one person in your educational establishment who will become your shoulder, just as you are a shoulder for so many others. Give it time, do not despair, and keep in mind that all will be well with time and patience.

Other principals out there have the same need as you. Almost all people need someone to talk to, and other principals have the same needs. No one understands your position as well as other principals, so it is advisable that this is where you turn.

According to Bill Hall, director of Educational Leadership and Professional Development in Florida's Brevard County school district, his county's mentors are self-selected. "Each principal-preparer picks their own mentor for various and personal reasons," he said. By allowing each principal-preparer the freedom to choose his or her own mentor, it takes some of the responsibility off the program director. More important, the choice assures principal candidates they are getting a mentor they will be comfortable confiding in.

To be uncomfortable at first in your new position is perfectly normal. Do not give up in the first or second year because in doing so, you are not giving yourself a fair chance. Take at least three to five years, allowing yourself time to adjust and learn how to manage, before deciding whether the position is right for you. You will most likely feel overwhelmed when you first step into the shoes of school leader and discover that your time is no longer your own, but everyone else's instead. As a principal, you will never please everyone, and this is not an easy fact to come to terms with. However, it can be done in time, once you have learned to adjust and accept that you are only one person. These feelings will pass in time, and it will only be a matter of months before your staff is welcoming a leader with passion, patience, caring, vision, and goals.

Know Your Limits

Everyone is an individual. As such, each person deals with stress in a different manner. Some people thrive on stressful situations, becoming more productive when their backs are against the wall, while others cave under the pressure. It is the same in all walks of life: Some writers do a better job when they are up against a deadline, while others fall apart and battle writer's block. Production workers may be able to produce more parts and meet their quota when they have only two hours of their shift left, while others will drop each part and falter under the pressure. You need to be aware of your personal limits and adjust your schedule and workload accordingly. If an eight-hour day is all you can handle at the office, delegate some of the work, and go home after eight hours have passed. You can always take paperwork home with you and delve into it after you have dinner and a few hours of relaxation.

Too much stress will eventually cause you to be working under emotional duress. This is not a good place to be, especially when dealing with an assortment of people, conflicts, or disciplines. It would be fine if you could lock yourself in the office and stay there until you have re-energized and are ready to face another five or six hours of constant demands. This is not a liberty you have, however, and you will not be able to use the hiding trick.

You must deal with each incident as it occurs, or on some days, deal with each incident by priority.

Many issues trigger stress, just as there are many factors that will determine how you deal with the daily and constant stresses of your position. Your level of self-esteem, possible personal problems, your personality and character traits, and your gender all determine how you handle stress.

Lynette J. Fields of the University of South Florida did a study on patterns of stress and coping mechanisms of school administrators. Her report stated that first-year principals and first-year assistant principals were most stressed by uncontrollable demands on their time, time taken away from their personal lives, prospective staffs, and conflict. The biggest stress relievers the principals and assistant principals were a sense of humor, exercise, and venting.

A sense of humor can get you through some extremely rough days. In Fields' study on first-years and assistants, more than 53 percent of first-year principals said they have found a sense of humor is the perfect mechanism to get them through their first year on the job. Some first-year principals and their assistants have found they can vent to one another, and the understanding between the two makes this a perfect union of friendship and harmony. Other first-year principals have admitted to enjoying playing practical jokes on their assistants, finding a humorous way to get through the day. "Positive reinforcement" was another release mechanism found by a first-year who decided to initiate a talent show in her middle school. Unlike most talent shows that take place in schools, it was the teachers who did the skits, and they made them humorous but educational. The students loved seeing their teachers, especially the tough ones, cutting up, and having fun, and the teachers had a good time coming up with the ideas and putting on a show for the kids.

A study in New Zealand found that 43 percent of surveyed principals reported that their stress levels over the previous week had been high or extremely high. The principals who reported being stressed were also high on the list of having illnesses, depression, anger, frustration, and having little to poor sleep. The high or extremely high stress levels were thought to be related to poor job satisfaction.

It is important that you know yourself well — your reactions to certain aspects of your job; your ability to handle those aspects; and which of those aspects has the worst affect on you mentally, physically, and emotionally. When you are feeling stressed, it is advisable to keep a journal, noting what happens on each day and what takes place that causes the stress. Once you see which tasks or conflicts cause you to get the most anxious or tense, you can begin looking for someone on your staff who can take over that particular responsibility or another way to cope with the stressor.

Burnout of principals is a great concern, and learning how to manage your stress can be beneficial to you, your staff, your students, your friends, and your family. Some possible positive outlets could be: getting away for a short weekend, reducing the number of events you attend, staying organized, not getting too far ahead of yourself, and taking one step at a time. Delegating jobs, having a confidante whom you can vent to, understanding that most people who are angry are not angry at you but at something or someone else, and not falling into the habit of procrastinating are other ways to keep the stress level at as much a minimum as possible.

Stress can cause depression, insomnia, increased blood pressure, rapid heartbeat, a decrease in the immune system, and countless other physical, mental, and emotional ailments. With the list of a principal's responsibilities growing longer and the hours to meet those additional responsibilities doing the same, principals now feel more pressure than ever. The secret to dealing with this insurmountable stress is learning how to survive — and remembering that your job as a principal is just that: a job. Here are some tips you can follow to help prevent burnout:

- **Do something for yourself that you enjoy**. Consider going to a festival, or going to a nearby river where you can walk, bike, or run. If you can afford to do so, reserve a hotel room with a hot tub or go camping. Whatever you decide to do, make sure it is something you enjoy.

- **Take up a hobby**. If you start a new hobby, you can share information about what you enjoy doing with your students, or try to incorporate it into one of your lessons during the year. This is also a great way to relax when you are not with your students. If there is something in your past that you have not done in awhile, like playing the piano or gardening, consider taking it up again for relaxation.

- **Get plenty of rest.** Sleep deprivation can lead to depression, lack of focus, anxiety, mood swings, and a negative attitude. Lack of sleep over a period of time can cause you to become run-down, your immune system will suffer, and you will become sick thanks to all the germs the students will expose you to.

- **Exercise and be active.** Not only does exercise allow you to vent frustration, but it also burns negative energy. You could join a gym, take yoga classes, swim, power walk, or run. A bowling league, softball team, or visiting a golf course may be your preference, and any of these are good choices for doing something you enjoy that is good for you both mentally and physically. It will also help you keep up with your students while you are at school.

- **Eat healthy meals and snacks**. Stress runs down your body, so it is important to eat healthily. Sometimes new principals will get so overwhelmed with the daily minutia of their jobs that they will skip lunch or work so late that the hunger passes. Do not do this to yourself; eating lunch is important for you physically. If you stay after school to get caught up on paperwork, remember to leave at a designated time.

On the Education World® website (**www.educationworld.com/a_ admin/admin/admin394.shtml**), you can find an article with 30 suggestions for principals dealing with stress. Laughter is the first suggestion listed. Another proposal is for principals to keep a praise file. Any compliment from a teacher, student, administrator, or parent, and any notes of praise written to you, should be kept in this file for future reference. It is advisable to pull out the file when you are feeling down or depressed because, in time, the number of notes will surprise you, and they will remind you that the good outweighs the bad. You can also surf the Internet, listen to music, spend time with the students, and read for fun. More suggestions that can help you deal with stress include enjoying nature, planning or cooking a meal, spending time with your pet, working in the garden, planning your time, doing things with friends outside of school, watching a favorite television show, and taking a weekend off.

The strategies you employ are completely up to you, but it is important that you do something to handle the stress of your job. The five tips above are a great guideline, while the more specific suggestions will be useful in giving you ideas for coping with your stress. Your family and friends will also help you deal with the demanding nature of your job; this is your built-in support system. Do not forget they are there, and do not take them for granted. Spend time with your family and friends, and remind yourself that they are also a priority. Have a date night with your spouse or significant other; take your kids to the park or rent a funny movie to watch with them; go out with your friends; or have a long conversation on the phone with your parents. Take the time for the important people in your life, and you will be rewarded in kind.

The reality is no matter how many books you read or how many people you talk to, there will be days that you will be unable to shake off the events that occurred during the day at work. Perhaps there was a confrontation with a parent, or one of your teachers approached you with a complaint, and the day only became worse from that point on. These are the days you may need to depend on your spouse or your best friend for his or her understanding ear or comforting shoulder. These are the days you might enter your home and immediately call your mother to complain about how horrible the day was. It is all right to vent to your family and friends on occasions such as these, and they will understand and be happy to be there for you. Just be sure not to go home night after night and do nothing but complain about the day you had. Everyone needs a sounding board, but if you use family and friends solely for this purpose on a daily basis and do not offer the same comfort in return, you might chase them away.

The coming crisis of having too few qualified principals is being felt in Australia as well as in the United States. A report by the Australian Council for Educational Research (ACER) stated that there were not enough applicants for becoming a principal due to stress and time demands of the job. Government educational departments all over the world are discovering that school leadership has an impact on learning, and with that knowledge as well as the shortage of upcoming principals, their attention has peaked. With the role of school principal having drastically changed over the past ten years, and the demands on school principals having become almost humanly impossible, people in high places are starting to take notice. Once it was determined that students learn better with a great leader, school principals and the demanding tasks placed on them began getting some attention. However, it will take time before anything is significantly changed for the better. On a good note, now you know there are things you can do to make your position easier to deal with.

Some people are natural worriers. If this is you, by all means, learn how to change that trait of your personality. Demands on principals are high enough without worrying needlessly. Worry causes health problems and raises stress levels. Do not waste valuable energy on trivial matters or issues that you have no control over. Make a list of the issues that you tend to worry about, then go back and look at them a few days later. Think about these issues, whether you have any control, and realize where you are wasting your strength, time, and energy.

"Have fun," said Oliver Phipps. "You have to have fun, or you'll burn out on this job. Whatever it takes to make it fun, do it, even if it is just sitting on the floor laughing with the kindergartners. If that is fun for you, then do it. Do it every day, if that is what you need."

The most important — and perhaps difficult — aspect of reducing stress is maintaining a positive attitude. Research by psychologist Martin Seligman of the University of Pennsylvania has proven that "optimistic people are happier, healthier, and more successful than those with a negative outlook on life." Everyone falls into a bad mood and becomes negative sometimes. It is human nature to react to bad days, but you can stop yourself from doing this by monitoring what you say and think. Attempt to think before you speak, and if you realize you are about to say something negative, stop yourself. If you find yourself feeling depressed, stop and adjust your thoughts. Instead of thinking about things that upset you, start thinking about the things in your life that make you happy, and push the negative thoughts out of your mind. You may not be able to control every aspect of your job, but you can control your responses to the stresses the day may bring.

Smile. Smiling is contagious, as is laughter, and most people around you will respond with the same. Look your colleagues in the eyes and smile, and then watch as they smile in return. An environment full of smiling and laughing people is a joyous place to be — for you, for your faculty and staff, and for your students.

Be proactive in taking care of yourself. Do not ignore your well-being; be sure make time for exercise and relaxation, and eat well — or at least eat enough. Spend time with your family and friends. Play, laugh, and have fun. Just because you are an adult does not mean you are no longer allowed to play. By doing what is necessary to relieve your stress, you will go into the school the next morning and be the successful, effective leader your school needs. At the same time, you will be taking care of yourself.

CHAPTER 10
Closing The Gap

To achieve and maintain a high level of leadership that is learning-centered, school principals must have support. This support must come from the school system, university, and state education leaders. These leaders must also have a good understanding of the present and future demands on every school and classroom. They must understand these demands to offer present and future leaders what is needed.

"Leadership has changed by light-years — tenfold," Bill Hall said. "I equate the change to golf [clubs], from hickory shaft to graphite."

The demands are endless, the time precious little, the importance of doing the job right, imperative. What is the future outlook for principals? "Principals and assistant principals cannot do it anymore," Hall said. "They need help. With accountability, legislation, social problems … one has to distribute accountability. The changes that must be made are in resourcefulness, time management, and money. There are always huge budget cuts, now on a large scale like never seen before. ... There has to be more resourcefulness."

With jobs leaving the country, tax dollars are shrinking at a rapid pace. This only means more budget cuts in education, leaving principals and superintendents on their own to find resources for their staff and schools. There are already thousands of teachers balking at the amount of money they must spend out of their own pockets to provide supplies for their students, and there are more cuts to come. If the teachers cannot afford to use their own money, and the principals have no funding for purchasing supplies or resources for their teachers, where will this leave the education of our children?

Another area of concern for future school leaders is ethics. "Brevard is very successful on programs for our school leaders, but in the future I see us having to look at how to model ethical leadership," Hall said. "There are too many instances of illegal and unethical activities in the schools of America today, such as sexual abuse. There are good people out there making stupid mistakes."

The demands are endless, and with the demands that are to come, there seems to be no limit in sight. What is the future outlook for principals? How does a first-year principal make the most of his or her leadership today and for years to come? The best way to attain success is to look where success is currently being achieved.

Measuring Success

After viewing the facts about these schools of excellence, perhaps you can look at your own school in a different perspective, seeing where things could possibly improve, if needed, or maybe garner a few ideas to continue on the road to success that your school is already traveling.

Once you take your position, if there are increases in complaints, students being moved to different schools, a decline in student performance and achievement, or staff members taking jobs at different schools, there is obviously a problem with your leadership. If your students are not learning, this is a measurement of your effectiveness as a school leader.

If, by chance, you find yourself in this situation, you need to question whether you have chosen the correct career. If you still feel that being a school leader is what you wish to do, find someone who can give you feedback on your performance as a leader. This person must be someone who is honest and not afraid of telling you the truth. That is the only way you will discover what you may or may not be doing wrong. If you do not have a mentor, find one. A mentor is an invaluable resource to improve your skills and can serve as your lifeline when needed.

A study in Canadian education reported the Edmonton Catholic schools held the best practices in education and excellence in student achievement. When glancing through the website of the Edmonton Catholic school district (**www.ecsd.net**), it is easy to see why they have been successful. They have numerous programs for students, staff, and parents available. One of their claims to excellence is that "teachers and principals take pride in our district because they share in the planning, decision making and student successes." Also, in Canada, the Alberta Board of Education established an "Accountability Pillar Report," a measure that gives all school boards in Alberta a consistent way to measure how well learning goals are achieved.

The Good Shepherd Catholic School in Santa Cruz, California, has a parent club. Their website states that all parents are members of the parent club. The principal of Good Shepherd, David Sullivan, trained for the principalship through the American Council on Education (ACE) Leadership Program at Notre Dame. Staff members at Good Shepherd said it is common to find Sullivan on the playground with the students during recess and lunch, taking part in their activities. They also said that he is a man who promotes the virtues of the community. "There is a growing absence of leadership in schools everywhere," Sullivan said.

Dr. Cassandra Hopkins is principal at River's Edge Elementary School in Georgia. Hopkins' mission is to educate students "through respect for self and others, expectations of excellence, envisioning the future, and superior education in a safe environment." Hopkins also states that the school staff and leader cannot be successful in their collective mission without the parents' assistance, "for successful parental involvement nurtures relationships and fosters partnerships." It is Hopkins' belief that it takes teachers, teacher assistants, administrators, and parents working together to produce children who are confident and lifelong learners. Hopkins also has a "my door is always open" policy.

Boston, Massachusetts, superintendent Dr. Thomas Payzant took on a district with more than 58,000 students, 4,700 teachers, and a district where 73 percent of the children live in poverty. Payzant attacked the problems head-on and shepherded a set of ongoing reforms called Focus on Children because he believes "American education will never improve for students if it is taken one school at a time." He stated that one of the most critical goals was refining strong school principals. Within Payzant's first year, he created a leadership team and has since established the Boston School Leadership Institute (**www.bostonsli.org**).

After dramatic gains in student achievement in the 2005-2006 academic year, 23 schools in the Plano, Texas, Independent School District (ISD) won the prestigious National Blue Ribbon School of Excellence honor. The Plano ISD mission and goals statement maintains "successful learning is best achieved through strong connections with parents, families, and all sectors of the broader community." The website for the Plano ISD (**www.pisd.edu**) is set up for easy access by parents, students, and staff, as well as others in the community. The Plano ISD superintendent, Dr. Doug Otto, was named one of the "21 Leaders for the 21st Century" by Inside Collin County Business. Otto is known as "one of the nation's leaders in educational technology, school administration, and school finance." Plano ISD's awards and honors are numerous, its mission to "ensure that all students are provided with an excellent education" — one they have obviously achieved.

The Collier County public school district in Florida has more than 45 percent of its students living in non-English homes, where English is not the first language and sometimes is not spoken; the district has met this challenge head-on. There are more than 6,700 students in its English Language Learners (ELL) program. The percentage of non-English homes rises to 54 percent in grades Pre-K through grade 3, the grade levels where learning to read is most critical. More than 57 percent of the student population is categorized as economically needy and qualify for free or reduced lunch.

The cultural diversity of the students in this district ranges from Caucasian, African American, Hispanic, Haitian, Asian, and Indian; because of the language barriers than can exist, the teachers, principals, school board, and superintendent have their hands full. Finding the means to communicate and then teach was a concern for many years. Collier County has had the ELL program in place since 1984 when the district had a total of 250 students enrolled, according to the school district's website (**www.collier-schools.com/about/fastfacts.asp**). In 2010, the ELL program had a total enrollment of more than 6,700 students. Nearly 54 percent of these students were enrolled in Pre-K through grade 3. Collier County's students speak 81 different heritage languages and come from 147 different countries of origin. Even with so much diversity, the district has a current graduation rate of 77.2 percent and a current dropout rate of 2.2 percent. The state grades the schools on an A+ Plan, and the district received an A at the end of the 2008-2009 school year. The district's school board states that "students are our number one priority, and their needs are the focus of all district decisions."

The six successful schools above are all focused on giving their students the best education possible, all having exceptional leaders with visions and goals and quality staff members who share those visions and goals. But there is one more school district to examine: Florida's Brevard School District. Brevard Public Schools received the 2007 Governor's Sterling Award for being a role model for excellence in organizational performance. Brevard District is only the second school district in Florida to receive this prestigious recognition.

Former superintendent Dr. Richard DiPatri oversaw the very diversified and distinguished Brevard Public Schools, which number 126 in all, for nine years before retiring in 2009 (He has since been named superintendent for Penn Foster Virtual High). In these educational establishments, there are more than 74,000 students ranging from pre-kindergarten through 12th grade. Of those students, more than 12,000 qualify for Exceptional Student Education (ESE) services. For more than 1,500 of the district's students, the primary language is one other than English. In 2008-2009, Brevard public schools had a graduation ratio of 94.7 percent and a dropout rate of 0.6 percent.

With the excessive number of students, the diversity of these students, the range of ages and disabilities of the "exceptional students," and the challenge of having students with limited English, DiPatri had every reason to be proud of his staff and student body at the time of his interview for this book. The key to running a successful school lies in DiPatri's attitude. "We work together as a team," he said.

Named Superintendent of the Year by the Florida Association of District School Superintendents in 2006, DiPatri leads by example. DiPatri has been called a "power-hitter" and a "visionary instructional leader." One board member credited DiPatri with having "laser-like focus on student achievement." DiPatri said that one of the most satisfying aspects of his job was developing school principals into instructional leaders.

Prior to becoming superintendent of Brevard County School District, DiPatri served in New Jersey as a teacher, coordinator, principal, superintendent of schools for Jersey City, deputy and assistant education commissioner, and state district superintendent of schools.

In reading over the monthly newsletters Dr. DiPatri has written, it is easy to see why he is such a well-known leader and exemplary role model. One newsletter headlined, "In Brevard Public Schools, the People Make the Difference." DiPatri is a strong believer in that everyone is part of each student's education. "The people who work on that team — from teachers and administrators to bus drivers and cafeteria workers — come to work every day ready to foster a positive environment for student achievement," DiPatri said.

As an exceptional leader, DiPatri never forgets that teaching students education and citizenship is attained through the team that is working together toward this common goal. Another newsletter written by DiPatri reads, "Thanks to the strong support of our school board, the hard work of our teachers, staff, administrators and district personnel, and the proactive involvement of our parents, we are laying the foundation for new levels of student achievement."

The vast amount of educational programs offered to the employees of the Brevard district, listed on the district's website **(www. brevard.k12.fl.us**), is phenomenal. There are programs for everyone, instructional and non-instructional employees alike. If anyone in the system wishes to educate and better themselves, Bill Hall — introduced in previous chapters as the district's director of educational leadership and professional development — is sure to offer the opportunity to do so.

In DiPatri's September 2007 newsletter, he wrote, "These days it is common knowledge that students whose parents are actively involved and concerned about their educational progress tend to have higher levels of achievement. Still, it never hurts to remind parents that the more engaged they are in their children's growth and development, the better chances they have of positively influencing their maturation into educated, contributing members of society."

DiPatri went on to write, "One hundred percent of the research studies upon which the campaign is based, compiled by The Parent Institute, indicate that parent involvement has a significant impact on student success." The campaign DiPatri refers to here is the "Be There" parent campaign at Brevard County Schools. "Be There" was first implemented in Volusia County after it was "agreed that parents play a critical role in the success of children and schools." Brevard schools started their "Be There" campaign in the fall of the 2007-2008 school year.

The newsletter of September of 2006 focused on safety. In that newsletter, DiPatri asked for the parents to help in keeping the children safe, writing that it "is all our responsibility — students, parents, teachers, and administrators — to be sure we are doing everything we can to keep our children safe and secure."

As a man of vision, DiPatri was aware of a problem looming on the horizon: the prospect of losing many seasoned principals as they approached retirement. Brevard was looking at losing as many as 15 principals at one time. DiPatri created a goal of preparing the district for the wave of retirements, unwilling to lose the massive experience these leaders would be taking with them. This was the start of his succession plan — the mentoring and training of future leaders. The amazing part of this plan is that it has evolved and is no longer just for principals, but for everyone "from cafeteria managers and childcare coordinators to ground supervisors and head custodians."

In looking ahead to this potential future problem, DiPatri saved the Brevard County district from what could have been a disaster. Losing many wise leaders at one time could have sent their students into a tailspin. DiPatri knew that, and he took the matter seriously. He and Hall prepared for the loss of their leaders by having those leaders mentor and train new blood. This program was not a new idea, but it was handled by two men willing to put in long hours and heartfelt caring to make it successful — and they took it further than most have ever considered.

CASE STUDY: WORD FROM THE EXPERTS

How Do You Judge Your Success?

- "With state testing such a priority, it would seem to reason that my success is based on student achievement. It could also be judged on teacher retention versus turnover. My success may also be judged on both the climate and condition of the school. I judge success by seeing students and staff grow. I want everyone to achieve more and learn more than the day before. I want them to do this because it is fun, not out of obligation." — **Tammy Brown**

- "My success will be judged based on the improvement students show on standardized tests, hands down. I measure my own success by improvement in test scores, professional growth of teachers, school culture and climate, satisfied parents, and happy students." — **Tret Witherspoon**

- **Oliver Phipps** measures his success "by the smiles on the kids' faces, by knowing they want to come to school, and by teacher retention, the staff wanting to come to work. We — principals — have to remember our staff has family. I tell them, 'Go home — be with your family.' Family comes first. The job will be here. If something happens to you and me, they will replace us. When all else fails, family is who will be there, and who you need."

- **Barbara Belanger** said she judges herself "by the success of goals met with students, teachers, and the community. If your school is a place where the community wants to gather, you have success."

- "I think a principal should measure his or her success by the climate or culture that ha s been created. The ideal would be to have a school culture in place where all teachers and staff believe they are responsible for the learning and success of all students."
— **Chet Sanders**

- **John Fielding** said to measure his success, he asks himself questions such as, "Are the kids learning? Is the staff happy? Do they all love kids? Do they love their jobs? Do the parents and others describe us as a friendly school?"

- "The satisfaction of the teachers and parents gauge my success and/or failure. My evaluations are exemplary; however, to me, the people I serve are my number one concern." — **Roy Miller**

Leadership and Mentoring

The goal of the leadership and mentoring programs in place at Brevard schools is to continue the direction in which the schools have been going under the present leaders. "Established learning communities are more likely to be disrupted or discontinued when a new leader steps into the principalship," Hall said. "Internal focus on the leadership sustainability can certainly counter this discontinuity of direction."

It has been proven that when a new principal takes his or her new role, if this leader is not open-minded and thoughtful in his or her steps to take the predecessor's place, the whole school community can be thrown into chaos and failure. "The continuity of direction that results from internal leadership development can preserve the core of a school or district's culture and allow it to stand strong against the buffeting winds of change despite new leaders taking over the helm," Hall said. "Schools and districts that do not put into place processes and structures that allow them to stay the course amidst changes in the individual leader are more likely to expose themselves to external change agents who could dismantle what is current practice. Internal leadership development can inoculate these organizations against any possible attack on their culture."

When Bill Hall was asked how Brevard was going to handle losing 15 valuable leaders in the near future, he said the district would do so "by using the senior staff, having the formal succession plan, leadership development, and by having the entire organization be a part of the succession plan. It is all about putting the process in place so everyone can be replaced with someone new and still have a high performing school district."

Hall said that most districts "focus just on senior leadership," but he believes in "building talent from within. Brevard has what they call the job family. That is, we look within the family, look at their skills, and map out a development plan with that in mind."

Knowing they had an oncoming disaster with the pending retirement of 15 valued leaders, Brevard called in a consulting firm "because we had no model to go by," Hall said. Instead of violating development, "we talked about succession planning, learned of a group out of Boca Raton, contacted them, and spent more than a year working on reports, ideas, and a solid plan based on best practice." The plan the consulting firm handed over was, "huge," Hall said. "It would have taken massive time, a complete overhaul, rethinking of philosophy. ... Instead, we decided to work with Human Resources and used feedback. We were still able to do our jobs. We decided to take on what we could do that made sense and was doable, roll out what we could, and put the plan in place."

"It is a road map," explained Hall of the leadership and mentoring program. "Working with the consulting firm added credibility to what we did." According to Hall, their ideas were fantastic, but not doable. The plan the district came up with instead was the one that has worked. Not only has it worked, but it has also led to other great plans that are being put into place.

The goal of the leadership program is Hall's vision. "It's what I think about at night instead of sleeping," he said. Hall believes that "instructional leaders have a moral obligation to ensure that our schools contribute to the sustainability of leadership in the profession. The best vehicle to carry out this moral imperative exists in the constructs of professional learning communities. We are morally obligated to pass the torch of leadership that was once passed to us. When you pass the torch of leadership, first make sure it is lit."

Hall said that the state had put management training in place in the late 1970s. The state provided funds and set up five regional programs. "This is what I grew up with," said Hall, who has been with Brevard Schools for 39 years, 16 of them in his current role. "The training the state offered was free, but they did away with it. We have tried to develop what we are doing through the idea of that program."

Hall believes there are six essential strategies to promote leadership sustainability:

- Create a formal leadership development plan.

- Develop a succession plan with a management component.

- Create a framework that provides for lateral and vertical capacity building.

- Develop a collaborative leadership team or guiding coalitions that support and promote distributed accountability.

- Put teachers into collaborative teams/professional learning communities (PLCs), and appoint one teacher as leader of each team.

- Make leadership development a specific essential job function on all administrative/supervisory job descriptions.

The leadership and mentoring program in Brevard County has its principal candidates in training before they actually assume leadership roles. They are certified for two years and then go through leadership training. Brevard County offers leadership and self-improvement programs all the time, for all its employees. Brevard has ten to 15 employees apply for the principal program each year — people who wish to improve their skills and are considering the position of principal in the future. These employees then transition to a formal coaching and mentoring program because "research bears out and has shown enhanced mentoring will be required," Hall said.

Hall said a succession plan is important because "without a succession plan, school districts could be: one promotion, one retirement, one demotion, one health-related incident, one winning lottery ticket away from disaster. Succession planning allows the momentum and inertia of existing leadership to continue long after the current leader is gone." It is safe to say that Brevard County's district leaders know and understand the value of great principals.

Bob Donaldson, a 46-year veteran principal who retired from Brevard Schools, came back to Brevard under contract to help new leaders succeed. Today he mentors new and recently appointed principals, offering help, advice, and guidance. What Donaldson offers is unique in that he has 46 years of experience to share.

"Bob works with, and mentors, the first-year principals for three years," Hall said. "He mentors, coaches, guides, and gives advice." Hall said what Bob and his first-year principals talk about is completely private, which keeps all first-years safe in their positions and, at the same time, "helps the administration learn what the first-year principals need to better themselves in their leadership. Bob cannot talk about any individual with anyone unless it is something illegal or immoral." This creates a trusting relationship between mentor and first-year principal.

Hall said the trust part of the mentoring program is important and gave an example of how this works: Say you are a first-year principal. You know you can trust Bob Donaldson, so you explain that you are frustrated with the budgeting for your school. Bob sees you need help in that particular area, so he makes a phone call to Hall and says, "Bill, we need a budgeting program." Hall then sets up classes for budgeting. Once the program is ready, Bob comes to you and says, "There is a new budgeting program being offered. Why don't you sign up for this?" This works for various reasons, and the outcome is success.

Hall said that you can perform a search on the Internet for succession planning and management, and you will find various sites having to do with corporate management and business. If you look for succession planning and management in public education, you will find nothing. "Succession planning should not and must not stand alone," Hall said. "It must be paired with succession management, which creates a more dynamic environment."

In order for you to do the best job possible, you need a mentor. There are those who are natural leaders, but even if you are one of those natural leaders, a mentor is a good confidante, a good friend, and the one person who will most likely save your sanity on those crazy and demanding days.

CASE STUDY: WORD FROM THE EXPERTS

The Biggest Challenges Faced by Today's Principals

- "I would love to have more time to get to know the families on a more personal level." — **Tammy Brown**

- **Katherine Munn** said her biggest challenge is "making everyone happy. It is an impossible task. I know that it cannot be done, but I want everyone to know that I do listen to their concerns and do the best that I can to solve problems."

- **Tret Witherspoon** said he has the hardest time "finding the time to complete all the day-to-day operations of being a principal."

- **Oliver Phipps** said the toughest aspect is "maintaining morale. There is always something, like a lack of funding, paperwork to keep organized, dealing with so many tests, laws, changes … It is hard to keep upbeat and stay focused. Another problem is maintaining the state assessment grade."

- **Roy Miller** said the hardest part of being a principal today is "the change in expectation from society as a whole. The school has now become a 'service center' that is expected to meet more than the academic needs of the children. We are bombarded with having to pick up where the parents leave off. This sometimes causes us to go into the lives of children far beyond the educational realm. I know teachers, at times, feel that they are more of a social worker than an educator."

- **Barbara Belanger** said the biggest challenge is "trying to maintain the position of instructional leader while often being out of the loop on curriculum and instructional materials. Much of this information is shared with assistant principals at their district meetings. As a principal, you have to really be proactive in keeping up with state-adopted materials and district assessments."

- **Barbara Belanger** said the biggest challenge is "trying to maintain the position of instructional leader while often being out of the loop on curriculum and instructional materials. Much of this information is shared with assistant principals at their district meetings. As a principal, you have to really be proactive in keeping up with state-adopted materials and district assessments."

- **Michael Miller** said the biggest challenge is dealing with the "accountability pressures from the high-stakes testing and just being able to keep up with everything you are in charge of. Just looking at the amount of paper that crosses my desk on a daily basis is overwhelming. Being able to keep track of where it came from, where you put it, and when it is due can be overwhelming. I have constantly looked to the one system that can organize me the best. I have come to the realization that I am probably the most organized of my friends."

- "The biggest challenge for first-year principals is securing and maintaining the confidence and trust from the public, faculty, and school district." — **James Gasparino**

- "The dynamic tension between the role of leader and manager is the greatest challenge. There is a need for visionary leadership in today's public schools, and the crisis management that is unavoidable can really get in the way unless a principal chooses his administrator team wisely; a combination of skills is needed to be able to develop and carry through with the vision while still maintaining or managing the day-to-day operation of the schoolhouse." — **Nancy Graham**

- **Barry Pichard** said the greatest burden is "parents' and community expectations. Parents and the community expect the schools to solve everything. Parents often expect the school to change their students because of their bad parenting skills. Parents have changed dramatically in the last five years. Before, I would have the students who were rude and disrespectful to teachers and school staff. Now the students are taking their cue from their best teachers — the parents, because they see them being rude and disrespectful to school staff when they are at conferences, meetings, et cetera. The community also blames all the social woes and problems on the schools because we are a good target. We do not defend our school enough when the public prints articles because the majority of our students come to school, do their work each day, have no problems, and earn scholarships, but the community sometimes only sees the students who make the newspaper or TV news."

- "The biggest challenge facing principals today is recruiting qualified teachers to work with our ever-changing student population. I work in a K-12 center school for students with emotional behavioral disabilities. There is an increase in students with severe problems who need teachers to meet their special needs."
  — Leonard Weiss

- **Chet Sanders** said the toughest challenge is "providing the leadership to develop in your teachers the desire to work collaboratively with each other to continually improve one another's practice."

- "I think the biggest challenge is finding the very best teachers that you can to meet the needs of your students. I will sometimes interview 30 teachers before finding just the right one that will fit the needs of a particular group of students. There were probably many of that group that will be good teachers, but for some reason I felt they were not a good fit. I tell teachers that a fair amount of my job is trying to keep the nonsense away from them. By nonsense, I mean things like politics, silly rules handed down from on high, all the extraneous things that the outside folks think would be a wonderful idea for schools — for example, every service club, environmental group, and charitable organization thinks a poster contest is a wonderful and original idea. In Florida, the Department of Education is constantly changing, and every change brings a fresh set of rules. Interestingly enough, almost none of them have any real impact on schools if the principal is willing to not get stressed by whatever they are saying. By the way, that is really hard — if not impossible — to do unless you have a supportive [school] board and superintendent above you." — **John Fielding**

- **John Redd** said the hardest part of principalship is "getting students to be motivated. This oftentimes is a result of their upbringing."

Future Outlook

In the future, Hall said he sees "better relationships with universities on what our principals need. We have to have communication, just as principals have to know how to communicate, how to budget, and they need more experience in many areas."

The state of Florida requires each school district to have a relationship with the universities and colleges in its service areas. Brevard is primarily working with the University of Central Florida and Nova Southeastern University, sending these universities data from its schools detailing what principals are missing and in what areas they are succeeding. In doing so, the schools hope to devise a way to better educate and prepare the principals of tomorrow. "Leadership has changed," Bill Hall said. "They are going to have to learn how to read data, learn how to use it, and be capable of data decision making. Principals need to partner with someone and get exposed to the data. Principals are now responsible for how well they do in creating capacity under their leadership. They have to develop leadership beneath them, and the people who are trained will be able to step in when it is time, or it is needed."

It is obvious that principals are no longer managers. "They are now expected to be instructional leaders first, managers second," Hall said. It is important for principals to stay on top of new technology and curricula, as there are more changes to come. With the many assorted hats you now wear, you must learn to make room in your closet for even more. However, with most states having the new leadership and mentoring programs, all the information provided to you here, and all the advice you have been given in the past, you are well on your way to being a good leader.

There have been numerous changes in the role of principal over the past ten years, but many anticipate that responsibilities will be even greater in the future. The National Association of Elementary School Principals (NAESP) began a project called Vision 2021. With this initiative, NAESP will "study the future of principalship, the trends and issues of what they think is to come. Digital learning technologies will change the way teachers teach and students learn." Some principals are wondering if technology will weed out brick-and-mortar schools, but other studies say the institutions still have multiple values people desire. Melanie Ward and David Newlands of Aberdeen University conducted a pilot study in 1998 and found that "Web-based learning does not substitute for face-to-face instruction." Dr. Bruce L. Mann, a professor of education at the Memorial University of Newfoundland, also conducted a pilot study in 1997 and followed up with the second part of the study in 2005, which led to the same conclusion.

Another requirement for today's principals is that they "globalize curriculum" so students can discuss worldwide issues. This concept gives principals something more to think about: the need to educate students on multiculturalism and inform them of issues and current events beyond that which happens in their own backyards. The focus on globalization can be incorporated into all basic academic disciplines. It is important that your students are aware of global events, worldwide cultures, and how these connect with their own lives.

Another major concern involves funding and budgets. With the nation having to address so many problems financially, the future of the schools and students is a major concern. Uneven per-pupil funding across the country is already a problem, but with jobs leaving the country, it looks like this will only continue to worsen. Another possibility for schools' and principals' future outlook is school-based management (SBM), which decentralizes control from the central district office to individual schools. More and more school districts are going with SBM, which puts more time-consuming burdens and decisions on the principals.

One thing to keep in mind is that even though there are going to be more responsibilities, it is now not only acceptable, but also suggested, that principals share the burden of those responsibilities. You do not have to do this alone. Legislatures, states, and district offices are finally admitting that, due to the amount of responsibilities, principals need assistants, and sometimes more than one. They are finally seeing the tremendous pressure principals are under, the demands they must meet, the stress from every angle that the position brings, and the need for assistants, which is now greater than ever before.

Although it is important that you stay focused on what is best for your students and school community, it is just as important that you remember to take care of yourself. Do not be afraid to ask for help and delegate responsibilities. This has become a necessity for all principals. Above all, you must learn how to share and delegate your many responsibilities — and, more important, know when it is time to quit for the day so you can take care of yourself and spend time with your family. With this in mind, and with the help of a caring mentor and exceptional staff, your first year as a principal can be a great success.

CASE STUDY: WORD FROM THE EXPERTS

Parting Pearls of Wisdom

- "It is a rewarding job. However, it is a job that takes a lot of time. You spend an enormous amount of time before and after school. You will have weekends when you must take things home. You will find yourself in the lives of your faculty. You will become their counselor in many ways. You must take time to listen. Also, I learned a long time ago that if they come to complain, they must also come with a solution where their complaint is concerned. If not, I just listen, and say, 'thank you.'" — **Roy Miller**

- "The best advice I can offer is to find a group of other principals you can use as your sounding board, to share experiences and gain knowledge. Meeting once a month with the group I am with has given me the feeling that I am not in this alone and that I need to trust my decisions. Principals need to remember not to forget their families and to make sure you have a balance between your professional and private lives." — **Barbara Belanger**

- "This is the most unrealistic job I have ever had with the demands and what I am responsible for that I have no say-so in, but it is also the most rewarding I have ever had. I had the opportunity to take a school from the bottom to the top. Test scores and morale were the lowest ever when I arrived, and now we are a model school that has achieved great scores — and at the same time, my teachers are happy. We work hard, but we play hard, also." — **Michael Miller**

- Go to work with a smile. Be out and about in your building. Work hard. Be professional. Get a good support team of fellow principals to call. Have fun every day. Make sure you take time for yourself. Remember that today is the best it is going to be. Tomorrow is another day, and you will get up and do it all over again knowing that today is the best it is going to be." — **Barry Pichard**

CONCLUSION

Now that you have a better understanding of what is expected of you and the responsibilities you will have as a school leader, you should be ready to enter your first year as a principal. At the end of the year, it is important that you reflect on the past school year. Looking back, you may find situations that you would have handled differently if you had only known what to expect or had more experience. You also may discover areas in the school you wish to improve that you did not think of at the start of the year. By using hindsight, you can plan for a less stressful and more successful year to come.

There are many ways to keep track of your first year so you can have a clear memory of everything that transpired and develop a comprehensive image of how you want to change things the following year. Keep a notebook on your desk so you can jot down thoughts and ideas as they occur. You can include notes about new programs you may wish to implement or a resource that may be good to look into. Remember the recommendation that you implement a journal? That can also be an invaluable tool as you reflect on the past year. You might also wish to survey your teachers and your students, either formally or informally, to find out if they have any suggestions or concerns for the upcoming school year.

As you reflect over the past year, try to look at yourself objectively. Reflect on your personality, your energy level, and how you did in communicating with students, teachers, parents, the community, the media, and your superiors. When you discover your strengths, you can assess how to best use them in your institution the following year. When you discern your weaknesses, you can devise a strategy to improve yourself and your methods to make your second year as a principal — and every year after that — even more successful than the first.

APPENDIX A

The Teacher Handbook: An Example

The following is an excerpt from John Fielding's teacher handbook for Idylwild Elementary School.

If you have ever been through a full interview with me, you know that I always give you a chance to ask anything you want. Most people, and everybody I have hired, have questions. Probably the most frequent is some version of, "What do you look for in teachers?" Although the specific words of my answer probably change, the basic philosophy does not. The short answer is that I look for someone who can do whatever job I'm interviewing you for better than I can, then try my best to give you what you need to be successful, and get out of the way. The next few paragraphs are the longer version of that answer.

I believe that it is important for you to understand that you have chosen what I believe is the most important profession of all. The Teacher Perceiver Interview defines "mission" as "a deep underlying belief that students can grow and attain self-actualization. A teacher with mission has a goal to make a significant contribution to other people." When I look for teachers, I look first for someone who displays a strong sense of mission. You must really believe in your heart that you are the most important person in changing a child, any child, into a productive adult. Any teacher who does not proudly display that belief should be selling shoes. My job as principal is to take teachers with mission and provide you with every possible resource to help you fulfill your mission.

One question on the TPI asks you to tell me what you believe an ideal school would be like. I think it is only fair that you know what I believe an ideal school would be like. In my ideal school everyone, from the youngest child to the oldest staff member, would be treated the same way you and I would like to be treated. Each person would be positive, encouraging, and empathetic with every other person. Everyone would feel successful in some way at the end of each day. Teachers would find ways to make each child believe that he or she was "teacher's pet." Teachers would constantly be looking for innovative ways to challenge students. They would always be trying to learn something new to improve their ability to help others both personally and professionally. Everyone would understand that listening skills are important and that you determine if you have been a good listener by looking to see if the speaker has been helped. Every teacher, every day, would be excited, not because they had done a good job of teaching, but because they had seen "a light come on" in each child. Every teacher would understand that even tiny little successes are important, and learn to build on them. Everyone would actively seek to build rapport with everyone else. Parents would be welcome and would look forward to coming to school.

If you have read carefully, you should have noticed that the most important things in my ideal school are relationships. Does that mean that I do not value good teaching, a strong, relevant curriculum, lots of resources, and pleasant surroundings? Of course not. However, I do not believe any of those things are possible without the positive relationships being in place first. Many of us have our own kids. You know the kinds of things you want them to learn. You want them to know how to get along with other people as well as all of the "book learning" that they will get in school. Each of you has an important role to play in helping our Idylwild kids learn to get along with others. Kids learn by watching adults. When they see you being helpful, kind, and courteous, they will model helpful, kind, and courteous behavior. If you allow your frustration to show and "act out," they will model that, too.

I invite you to share my vision of an ideal school by working first and hardest on building a strong, positive rapport with every student, each other, other staff members, and parents.

APPENDIX B

Word from the Experts

Implementing New Curricula in Your School

- "First, teachers are asked to look at the materials and maps before implementing. Teachers are encouraged to help write curriculum maps for the district as well as serve on district curriculum teams and provide input. Our school has curriculum committees to support each other in implementation as well. Advice to others in implementing new curriculum: Involve teachers in decision making and exploration as much as possible. Provide training in curriculum mapping as needed." — **Tammy Brown**

- "When the district chooses a new curriculum, they offer extensive in-services for that new curriculum. Advice to others in implementing new curriculum: Let the teachers have input so they are stakeholders, and be sure that there is plenty of opportunity for staff development of the new curriculum." — **Katherine Munn**

- "I would recommend doing an environmental scan of your present school's curriculum to see what works and what doesn't work. There may not be a need for a complete overhaul. Next, I would talk with other school principals and curriculum directors to see what works for them and why. Networking is always key."
  — **Tret Witherspoon**

Why They Became Principals

- "As a teacher, I didn't set out to be a principal but often found myself in leadership roles. I had a principal who saw that in me and encouraged me. I was intrigued by the idea of being able to reach more students by reaching teachers. I love people!" — **Tammy Brown**

- "Ever since my first day of teaching, I knew that I wanted to be a principal. I don't know why — it was just my dream." — **Katherine Munn**

- "By serving as a principal, I am able to have a greater impact on the learning by involving all stakeholders and generating a nurturing school culture and climate." — **Tret Witherspoon**

How They Define Their Roles as Principals

- "My role is, first and foremost, that of an instructional leader, guiding staff through the process of analyzing data and creating engaging lessons for students. Of course, there are numerous roles that must be fulfilled as well: communication with stakeholders — staff, community, parents, and students — to keep us working as a team, manager of resources and personnel, maintenance of facility, and working closely with custodial and trades people to have quality facilities." — **Tammy Brown**

- "I feel that I am the curriculum leader of the school. I am a facilitator and mediator between parents, community, faculty, and staff." — **Katherine Munn**

- "I would describe myself as the instructional leader of my school. I am also in charge of maintenance, discipline, school improvement, et cetera." — **Tret Witherspoon**

Words of Wisdom that Helped the Veterans Through Their First Years as Principals

- "I had a very good principal when I was an assistant principal. He was a great mentor. He helped me understand budgeting and formulas for the hiring process. He taught me what to look for in a teacher. 'Look for the heart,' he told me. My dad, also a principal, always talked to me and told me to treat people with respect — even when critiquing their work, do it in a respectful way. Help them instead of belittling them." — **Oliver Phipps**

- "My director told me that the decisions that I make would take as long as 20 minutes my first year. However, as I began to build a 'database' of answers to questions, within a few years, those same questions would be answered in as little as three seconds." — **Roy Miller**

- "Call before you act. It is always easier to get advice than to clean up a mess." — **Michael Miller**

- "There are very few decisions that have to be made immediately. Stop what you are doing when someone walks in your office to see you. Their issue matters to them, and they need your undivided attention." — **Nancy Graham**

- "Make sure you take time for yourself, because you will need it. You cannot run on all cylinders 24/7." — **Barry Pichard**

- "Respond to all communications, such as e-mail and phone calls, on the day you receive them." — **Robert Spano**

- "Never be bullied into making a decision before you have all the facts. Delay immediately solving a problem; it may not be one tomorrow. Treat everyone as an individual. This too shall pass." — **Leonard Weiss**

- "If it is good for kids, the answer is yes." — **Chet Sanders**

- "Make a friend with another administrator and be able to share experiences. Make sure you open up to your spouse and not let things get bottled up once you go home." — **John Redd**

- "Remember that you usually have made a situation a lot worse in your head then it actually is." — **Barbara Belanger**

- "Some advice that I found valuable is to realize not to avoid problems. They will not go away and probably become worse." — **James Gasparino**

- "The day will not last forever. Focus on the kids."
  — **Pamela C. Mitchell**

How Important Are the Teachers in Your Success as Principal?

- **Oliver Phipps** said teachers are "very important. Use all their gifts because one person cannot do it all. If you have a teacher who is good at PowerPoint® presentations, use them for it, and give them recognition. My dad told me, 'What is a leader? A servant.' Make sure your teachers have everything they need to keep afloat."

- "The school sinks or swims with the faculty that is in place in the building." — **Roy Miller**

- "My teachers are the most important people on my campus. They are the ones that students and parents see and communicate with first in any situation. When hiring, you need to remember that the abilities of enthusiasm, commitment, and teamwork are high on the priority list. Most other abilities can be taught." — **Barbara Belanger**

- "My teachers are very important. Even though the students are my priority, I could not fulfill my priorities without the cooperation from my teachers. I always look for the best in each teacher. I treat them as I would a student — not one is perfect, and if you look for the positive, you will find it. I place my teachers in a position and environment that best suits them so that they can be the best that they can be. I do not believe in forcing teachers to teach something that they do not want to teach, or be a part of a committee they do not want to be a part of. It took me four years to get that understanding across to my teachers, and I rarely run into resistance. If I do, I can usually reach a compromise." — **Pamela C. Mitchell**

* "They are the most important thing to student performance in the classroom. I told my teachers the first day on campus there would be millions of times I would rely on them to make the decision. Then there would be times I needed to make a decision, and I would need their input before I made my decision. Lastly, there would be times I would have to make a decision, and they would have to have the faith that I was doing what I thought was best." — **Michael Miller**

* "Teachers are the heart of the matter in a school. I am currently working with my staff to become a 'strengths-based' organization using the research from Gallup to better capitalize on the natural talents of folks instead of trying to force skills or abilities that may really just be unavailable." — **Nancy Graham**

- "Teachers make it happen or not happen. They are in the trenches every day. They are the communicators with the parents on a daily basis. Students do better when they feel that their teacher respects them. In order to earn respect, you have to give it first. So when teachers are professional and use good judgment, it makes my job a lot easier." — **Barry Pichard**

- "Teachers are the most important staff members in your building. They can work as a team and learn from one another." — **Robert Spano**

- "Teachers are the foundation of any school. You must recognize individual strengths and use them to increase student achievement. You will have prima donnas who are excellent teachers. A good principal will work with them." — **Leonard Weiss**

- "Teachers are our most important resource by far. The second-most is not even close. It is critical that I learn their strengths and where they will be most effective." — **James Gasparino**

- "Teachers are the main ingredient in any good school. You have to give them a little direction, and then let them go and do their thing. Encouragement is something they need a lot of, and you should find a way to see they have what they need to do their jobs right." — **John Redd**

Challenges Caused by the Previous Principal

- "The previous principal was there so long, and the staff had been with him a long time. If you make changes, they say, 'We used to do it this way.' You have to try to get people to share your vision. You have to win them. Change scares people." — **Oliver Phipps**

- "The most difficult challenge was to overcome the perception that a female could not do the job. At five-foot-four, I hardly matched the [previous principal's] towering six-foot-plus stature, and the perception [was] that I could not handle a school so large with so many issues. I am a tough cookie from Brooklyn, New York, and grew up with five other siblings." — **Pamela C. Mitchell**

- "The hardest [challenge] was working to get out of debt in our internal budget as well as with our school advisory board budget." — **Barbara Belanger**

- "The person before me had to make all the decisions. I had to teach my faculty how to make decisions." — **Michael Miller**

- "In one school, it was helping the kids understand that they were no longer in charge. In another school, it was helping the adults understand that children deserve to be treated with respect. In one school, it was redirecting the focus on instruction rather than athletics and/or tradition. And in yet another, it was helping teachers understand that when they fight against the bigger organization — the school system — they are ultimately beating up themselves." — **Nancy Graham**

- "When I went to my first school, the easiest challenge was that I was visible. The previous principal was not out-and-about at duty, lunch duty, walking the halls, visiting the classrooms. Teachers, children, and parents started noticing this right away, and I have kept this strategy at my new school that I have just opened. You must be visible. The hardest thing is always the saying, 'This is how it has been done before,' and as a new principal, you must be ready to expect this. Teachers are creatures of habit."
  — **Barry Pichard**

- "The principal before me had a laissez-faire attitude toward staff professional policies such as being to work on time, sick leave, planning, et cetera. When I became principal, it was apparent that I had to develop a staff handbook which outlined professional practices for teachers and staff." — **Leonard Weiss**

- "The reason I was appointed principal at my current school was that my predecessor allowed the school to become divided. Teachers, parents, and the PTO sided either for or against her. It became so bad that there were demonstrations, and people wore different-colored ribbons to indicate their allegiance. The school had gone through three different principals in seven years. It was my job to unite the school community. I am finishing my fifth year there now and will be returning next year." — **James Gasparino**

- **Chet Sanders** said his toughest challenge was "changing the culture of the adults in the school. Typically, the principal will dictate the school's culture, and that is the hardest single area to change."

The Most Rewarding Part of Being a Principal

- **Oliver Phipps** said the most rewarding aspect for him was "having staff members who do not want to leave. Some numbers [of teachers] went down after I started the position as principal, but they had to leave, even though they did all they could to stay. Seeing smiles on the staff's faces, that is rewarding."

- **Barbara Belanger** said her favorite aspect of her position is "being able to develop goals and design strategies to meet those goals. It is very rewarding to have a vision for your school, making it known to all the stakeholders, and having everyone, parents, students, and staff work together to accomplish your goals."

- **Pamela Mitchell** said she most enjoys "helping students realize some level of success for the first time. As an example, I worked with a student who was an underachiever — academically and behaviorally. He was failing all of his subjects, had scored at the lowest level on standardized tests, and had very low self-esteem. I taught him a reading strategy and asked him to research the strategy, teach it to others during his lunch time, and then prepare a Power-Point to present to teachers during a faculty meeting. He went for broke — scored at or above grade level on all of the standardized tests in the eighth grade, passed eighth grade, and surprised me with a note in the yearbook that stated that he was most thankful for that experience. Students who show progress and reach a level of success that they did not have before are the most rewarding experiences any principal could have."

- **Michael Miller** said he likes to "see how much my teachers have grown and seeing such a rise in student performance. I was able to take a school everyone in the district made fun of to one where more than 20 schools from around the state came to visit last year. I believe my job is to make a teacher be the best they can be, and I am constantly amazed at how far my teachers have come. There is nothing they cannot accomplish."

- **Robert Spano** said he most appreciates "when I see a child be successful and know that my staff enjoys coming to work each day."

- "My most rewarding experience was when our school became a Title I Choice School, whereby parents from failing schools could opt to send their children to us. Many feared that this would result in a decline in our academic achievement. Instead, our test scores went up, and two years later, we were recognized as the 15th top-performing elementary school in the state of Florida."
— **James Gasparino**

- **Chet Sanders** said the best part of his job is "creating a school climate that is warm and caring for all students, but still maintains high expectations for their ability to perform high-level tasks."

- "The kids have been the most fun through the years. I get a new batch of them every year, and I get to meet so many kids that are nice people." — **John Redd**

Things They Feel Should Be Changed in the Education System

- "Testing — there is too much, too much stress. Accountable is fine, but the testing is too much. We have two weeks of testing. They should cut it back and let us teach, especially in elementary. Let them be children. The children need to learn to play, to socialize. Corporations put people in cubicles — take the cubicles away and you get cooperative teaming." — **Oliver Phipps**

- "Pay for teachers needs to be on par with other professionals that we entrust with our most precious national resource: children. It is difficult to reconcile the notion that teachers continue to go into teaching for the love of it when they have families to support, and gas prices are reaching four dollars a gallon.

  "Eliminate any merit pay system for teachers. Children are not cars, real estate, or stocks. We should not be paid 'extra' for helping kids realize success. That is why we get paid in the first place. Raise salaries, and we would attract the best individuals, and more important, keep them.

  "Eliminate tenure. Have you ever seen the work ethic, loyalty, and care leave so fast in some individuals [as] when they get tenured? The teachers' union becomes their passion, and the administration their target. Students become a distant memory." — **Pamela C. Mitchell**

- "University teaching preparation has failed to keep up with the needs of public schools. Lip service of legislators needs to become action in regards to the importance or value of educators. Valid, researched, real-life data needs to drive decisions." — **Nancy Graham**

- "I tell my teachers that parents and community members have high expectations of school employees: teacher, administrator, or support staff. In order to be respected, you must earn respect. We have not done a great job in the arena because we often do not communicate with parents when needed, or some of our fellow professionals commit some type of crime that mars our entire profession. Then everyone dumps us into the same basket with all the bad apples. I think this is why many folks are looking to other types of schooling. We will always have these folks in our profession, but we need to celebrate and let our communities know the school system is the greatest in the world.

"I think we should give all students a free lunch, also. My school provides a free breakfast to any student who wants it. I realize it would cost the government some money, but the ones who suffer are the middle- to lower-income families that do not qualify for free and reduced lunch. Many a teacher and I have paid for or loaned money to students so they would not go hungry during the day. Students get upset in the morning when they have forgotten their lunch money and know they are not going to get anything to eat. Even though we have a system in place to prevent this at my school, they still feel upset. If the legislatures want to discuss a break for families, this may be a start.

"I am all for accountability of my students, staff, et cetera. However, the "A" word has taken on a whole new profile. Legislators, state boards of education and the U.S. Congress are making the rules and guidelines, but many of neither them — nor their staffers — have been in a school to even see what goes on each day. No Child Left Behind has not only left children behind, but also has left teachers, administrators, support staff, parents, and communities behind. The program makes good press, but when money is not linked with legislation to impact a program, then the program needs to be placed on the back burner until funding can fully support this program for a ten- to 20-year period, with increases in the funding as more students and staff enter that school." — **Barry Pichard**

- "The grading of schools [and] funding of schools. Providing more alternative placements for kids that are a constant disruption to the educational setting. It should be a privilege to attend a school, and if you abuse that privilege, then an alternative setting should be provided." — **Robert Spano**

- "School grading policies are unfair in most cases. For the most part, low-performing schools have very low parent involvement, students who live at the lower end of the socioeconomic scale and live in single parent homes. The deck is stacked against these schools.

"In order to increase salaries, teacher tenure practices and how teachers are paid will have to be revised. First of all, every tenured teacher should have a thorough evaluation every three to five years to determine if their contract should be renewed. In most cases, [a] gain [in] scores and other measures that determine student growth would be evaluated. If science and math teachers are in demand, we should pay them more. Most teacher salary schedules now are based on years of experience, degree, and not anything else. We need different salary schedules for teachers depending on what they teach.

"No Child Left Behind … is far too punitive and punishes educators for variables they cannot control related to student achievement. I have no problems with educators being held accountable for student performance. However, the playing field is not level in terms of socioeconomic status, student transience, and support for education by parents." — **Leonard Weiss**

- "One thing that should be changed is the way we evaluate schools. Accountability is important and necessary. However, it should be based on more than one test score. Another is funding for schools. Public money should not be diverted to private schools. Lastly, we have to do a better job in reclaiming public trust." — **James Gasparino**

- "In general, I think we are placing way too much emphasis on high-stakes tests. I do not mind being accountable for student growth, and some of the testing which has been implemented in the last several years has actually been beneficial and improved teaching and learning. But we have also made a bunch of kids and grown-ups a bit neurotic with the pressure." — **John Fielding**

- "The curriculum needs to reflect the knowledge and skills that are required by the 21st century global economy. We need to increase the depth of understanding rather than 'covering' material. We need to help students see the connections between big ideas and bodies of knowledge rather than teaching isolated disciplines. Instruction should aim for authentic tasks in real-world settings."
  — **Chet Sanders**

Advice Concerning Standardized Testing

- "Do not play it up. That is too much pressure on the kids and parents. Teach the standards and curriculum and all will be fine." — **Oliver Phipps**

- "Teach the standards, state and local. Make sure your faculty knows what is expected of them. Continue to review the data, and look for ways to improve." — **Roy Miller**

- "Make sure your teachers understand the standards they are to be testing, and meet with them frequently to monitor progress. Support standardized testing even though you may not always agree with it." — **Barbara Belanger**

- "Be positive about it. Do not get hung up in the drama. Use the data to drive your school's curriculum — stay focused on the kids." — **Pamela C. Mitchell**

- "Forget the test; focus on the standards; be willing to be accountable; and hold the same level for your teachers." — **Nancy Graham**

- "Give teachers in-service on administration and interpretation of tests to ensure validity and reliability. Make sure special education teachers review IEPs for accommodations." — **Leonard Weiss**

- "Whether we like it or not, standardized testing is the way our schools are judged. First-year principals need to become proficient in analyzing student performance data, and use it to improve instructional programs." — **James Gasparino**

- "It is extremely important that all teachers have their curriculum aligned to the standards that are being assessed. Instructional calendars and curriculum mapping are essential." — **Chet Sanders**

APPENDIX C

More Resources

U.S. Department of Education (**www.ed.gov**) — The U.S. ED offers a wide range of resources for principals, including pertinent news and feature articles, information on grants and funding, research and statistics, and a database of education-related government programs.

The Principal Story (**www.wallacefoundation.org/principalstory**) — *The Principal Story* is a national PBS broadcast film and media outreach project. Funded by The Wallace Foundation, the documentary and its related video and print materials are designed to connect educators and policymakers to reliable, useful, and free resources.

National Association of Secondary School Principals (**www.principals.org**) — The NASSP website includes a helpful knowledge center and free publications targeted toward school improvement.

National Association of Elementary School Principals (**www. naesp.org**) — The NAESP provides a wealth of research-based information and "promising practices" other principals have implemented in their own schools that you can use to improve your institution.

American Association of School Administrators (**www.aasa.org**) — The AASA has a host of publications specifically for school administrators, including a monthly magazine, a quarterly journal, books, newsletters, "toolkits," and research papers.

Accommodations Manual: How to Select, Administer, and Evaluate Use of Accommodations for Instruction and Assessment of Students with Disabilities (**www.ccsso.org/content/pdfs/Accommodations-Manual.pdf**) — This manual outlines a five-step process developed by the Council of Chief State School Officers (CCSSO) State Collaborative on Assessment and Student Standards Assessing Special Education Students.

Free Newsletters (**www.wrightslaw.com/links/free_nwltrs. htm**) — A comprehensive list of free newsletters put together by Wrightslaw covering a variety of topics.

Stop Bullying Now! (**http://stopbullyingnow.hrsa.gov/adults/ teachers-corner.aspx**) — Developed by the U.S. Department of Health and Human Services' Health Resources and Services Administration, the DVD toolkits include animated Webisodes that depict how students experience bullying and reach safe and healthy solutions; public service announcements; video workshops for professionals in education; and an instructor's guide to help teach children about bullying.

International Bullying Prevention Association (**www.stopbullyingworld.org**) — Includes a plethora of resources, research, training, and "best practices."

The Cyberbullying Research Center (**www.cyberbullying.us**) — A comprehensive resource for dealing with the newest form of bullying, this website includes a plethora of research, videos, articles, and a blog.

Scholastic Administrators (**www.scholastic.com/administrator**) — This website offers great ideas and resources for school administrators.

Teacher-to-Teacher Workshops (**www.paec.org/teacher2teacher**) — Developed by the ED, you can recommend these workshops to your teachers for staff development.

Education World (**www.educationworld.com/a_admin**) — This website's administrator section provides an impressive archive of resources, articles, and information relating to any possible topic of interest to school administrators.

ISLLC Standards (**www.ccsso.org/content/pdfs/isllcstd.pdf**) — As discussed in the text of this book, these are the guidelines you are expected to follow as a principal. Review them free here.

National Center for Educational Statistics (**http://nces.ed.gov**) — The NCES is the primary federal entity for collecting and analyzing data related to education.

Office of Educational Technology (**http://ed.gov/technology**) — The OET's School 2.0 eToolkit provides the resources for you to bring your school up to speed in its use of technology in the classroom.

Federal Resources for Educational Excellence (**www.free.ed.gov**) — FREE offers myriad teaching and learning resources you can implement in your school.

American Institute of Stress (**www.stress.org**) — AIS offers comprehensive research and reports on job-related stress as well as tips for stress management.

The National Youth Violence Prevention Resource Center (**www.safeyouth.org/scripts/topics/school.asp**) — The NYVPRC provides articles, fact sheets, best bets, and other resources for the prevention of school violence.

BIBLIOGRAPHY

American Community Survey. "Population and Housing Narrative Profile: 2008," U.S. Census Bureau, accessed February 9, 2010, **http://factfinder.census.gov/servlet/ NPTable?_bm=y&-qr_name=ACS_2008_1YR_G00_NP01&- geo_id=01000US&-ds_name=ACS_2008_1YR_G00_&-_ lang=en&-redoLog=false**.

Anderson, Nick, and Shear, Michael D. "A $4 Billion Push for Better Schools," *The Washington Post*, July 24, 2009, accessed February 19, 2010, **www.washingtonpost.com/wp-dyn/con- tent/story/2009/07/23/ST2009072303922.html**.

Armistead, Lew. "Public Relations and the High School Princi- pal," Spring 2007, accessed February 28, 2008, **www.princi- palspartnership.com/feature1003.html**.

Baumel, Jan. "Understanding Special Education Laws and Rights," Great Schools Inc., June 9, 2006, accessed March 12, 2008, **www.schwablearning.org/articles.aspx?r=78**).

Bergman, Abby Barry. *A Survival Kit for the Elementary School Principal: With Reproducible Forms, Checklists, and Letters*. Paramus: Prentice Hall, 1998.

Brock, Barbara L., and Grady, Marilyn L. *Launching Your First Principalship: A Guide for Beginning Principals*. Thousand Oaks: Corwin Press, 2004.

Buck, Amanda, and Powell, Mickey. "New round of budget cut proposals hit schools," *The Martinsville Bulletin*, February 18, 2010, accessed February 18, 2010. **www.martinsvillebulletin. com/article.cfm?ID=22533**.

Center for Union Facts. "Protecting Bad Teachers," Teachers Union Facts, accessed February 17, 2010, **http://teachersunion-exposed.com/protecting.cfm**.

Chea, Terence. "Schools face big budget holes as stimulus runs out," The Associated Press, February 15, 2010, accessed February 17, 2010, **www.google.com/hostednews/ap/article/ALeqM5g-zSA5JFSmT_ACkqwW17RWpABeY7gD9DS59V80**.

Chereb, Sandra. "Bigger education cuts surprise Nevada lawk-makers, teachers union, as special session looms," The Associated Press, February 18, 2010, accessed February 18, 2010, **www.businessweek.com/ap/financialnews/D9DUM26G0. htm**.

Collier County Public Schools. "District Profile," District School Board of Collier County — Fast Facts, February 18, 2010, accessed February 18, 2010, **www.collierschools.com/about/fastfacts.asp**.

Cravits, Cathy. "Do You Have What it Takes To Be a School Principal?" EZine Articles, September 21, 2007, accessed April 17, 2008, **http://ezinearticles.com**.

Cusick, Philip A. "A Study of Michigan's School Principal Shortage," Michigan State University, N.D., accessed April 20, 2008, **www.epc.msu.edu/publications/REPORT/REPORT.pdf**.

Dillon, Sam. "Obama to Seek Sweeping Change in 'No Child' Law," *The New York Times*, January 31, 2010, accessed February 17, 2010, **www.nytimes.com/2010/02/01/education/01child. html**.

_____. "Wi-Fi Turns Rowdy Bus Into Rolling Study Hall," *The New York Times*, February 11, 2010, accessed February 17, 2010, **www.nytimes.com/2010/02/12/education/12bus.html**.

DiPatri, Richard A. "In Brevard Public Schools, the People Make the Difference," February 2008, accessed April 14, 2008, **www. brevard.k12.fl.us**.

Edmonton Catholic School District. "Dealing With Parent – School Conflict Management," 2008, accessed March 27, 2008, **www.ecsd.net/parents/conflict_managment.html**.

Einhorn, Erin. "Teachers in trouble spending years in 'rubber room' limbo that costs $65M," *The Daily News*, May 4, 2008, accessed February 14, 2010, **www.nydailynews.com/ ny_local/education/2008/05/04/2008-05-04_teachers_in_trouble_spending_years_in_ru.html**.

Gentile, Carmen. "Student Suspended for Facebook Page Can Sue," *The New York Times*, February 16, 2010, accessed February 17, 2010, **www.nytimes.com/2010/02/16/education/16student. html**.

Goldman, Russell. "Utah Lawmaker Seeks to Eliminate 12th Grade," ABCNews.com, February 16, 2010, accessed February 17, 2010, **http://abcnews.go.com/WN/ utah-mulls-eliminating-12th-grade/story?id=9853553**.

Good Shepherd Catholic School. "General Info, Principal," 2007, accessed April 7, 2008, **www.gsschool.org/general_principal. html**.

Grimes, Cathy. "Governor's proposed K-12 budget cuts hit school breakfast programs and coaches' salaries," *The Daily Press*, February 17, 2010 accessed February 18, 2010, **http:// articles.dailypress.com/2010-02-17/news/dp-local_ga-cross- over-impact_02feb18_1_breakfast-programs-budget-cuts- districts**.

Gutierrez, Bridget. "Principals: How Important Are They?" *The Atlanta Journal-Constitution*, November 27, 2007, accessed April 18, 2008, **www.aja.com/blogs**.

Hopkins, Cassandra. "Principal's Message," Rivers Edge Elementary School, N. D., accessed March 8, 2008, **www.clayton. k12.ga.us/schools/129/principal.html**.

Hopkins, Gary. "The Best and Worst Things About Being a Principal," Education World, 2001, accessed March 12, 2008, **www. educationworld.com/a_admin/admin/admin253.shtml**.

Kohut, Margaret R. *The Complete Guide to Understanding, Controlling, and Stopping Bullies & Bullying: A Complete Guide for Teachers & Parents*. Ocala: Atlantic Publishing, 2007.

Kumar, Anita. "In private, Virginia governor pushes deep budget cuts," *The Washington Post*, February 17, 2010, accessed February 17, 2010, **www.washingtonpost.com/wp-dyn/content/article/2010/02/16/AR2010021605819.html?hpid=sec-metro**.

Lambert, Lisa. "Obama outlines new education vision in budget," Reuters, February 1, 2010, accessed February 16, 2010, **www.reuters.com/article/idUSN0119881420100201**.

_____. "States to government: hands off education," Reuters, February 1, 2010, accessed February 16, 2010, **www.reuters.com/article/idUSTRE6100S920100201**.

Lizma, Juan Antonio, and Slayton, Jeremy. "Mobile devices said to be the next wave in education," *The Richmond Times-Dispatch*, February 15, 2010, accessed February 16, 2010, **www2.timesdispatch.com/rtd/news/local/education/article/MOBI15_20100214-222004/324357/**.

Lusebrink, Chantelle. "Court prods state to provide more dollars for education," *The Issaquah Press*, February 16, 2010, accessed February 17, 2010, **www.issaquahpress.com2010/02/16/court-prods-state-to-provide-more-dollars-for-education/**.

Marlow, Stacey, and Minehira, Norman. "Principals as Curriculum Leaders: New Perspectives for the 21st Century," Pacific Resources for Education and Learning, N.D., accessed February 15, 2008, **www.prel.org/products/Products/Curriculum. htm**.

National Association of Elementary School Principals. "Vision 2021," NAESP ONLINE, Spring 2007, accessed April 7, 2008, **www.vision2021.org/anticipating_the_future_.html**.

National Center for Education Statistics. "State & County Estimates of Low Literacy," National Assessment of Adult Literacy, accessed February 9, 2010, **http://nces.ed.gov/naal/estimates/overview.aspx**.

The Ohio Association of Elementary School Administrators. "OAESA Mission." OAESA Brochure, N.D., accessed April 1, 2008, **www.oaesa.org/brochures/whome.pdf**.

_____. "OASSA Mission." OASSA Update, August 2004, accessed April 4, 2008, **www.oassa.org/**.

Phillips, John Arul. "Manager - Administrator to Instructional Leader: Shift in the Role of School Principal," Faculty of Education, University of Malaya, N.D., accessed March 3, 2008, **www.peoplelearn.homestead.com/principainstructleader. htm**.

Phillips, Rich. "Facebook gripes protected by free speech, ruling says," CNN.com, February 16, 2010, accessed February 16, 2010, **www.cnn.com/2010/TECH/ptech/02/16/facebook. speech.ruling/index.html**.

Plano Independent School District. "2008-2012 Strategic Plan," About Us, accessed April 4, 2010, **www.pisd.edu/about.us/ mission.goals/index.shtml**.

Ricken, Robert, Terc, Michael, and Ayres, Ida. *The Elementary School Principals Calendar: A Month-by-Month Planner For the School Year*. Thousand Oaks: Corwin Press, 2006.

Rubenstein, Grace. "Pyzant on Principals: Key Players in School Reform," *Edutopia*, June 2006, accessed April 4, 2008, **www. edutopia.org/payzant-principals**.

Schmidt, Laurel L. *Gardening in the Minefield: A Survival Guide for School Administrators*. Portsmout: Heinemann, 2002.

Silva, Cristina. "Class size amendment moves forward," TampaBay.com, February 17, 2010, accessed February 18, 2010, **http://blogs.tampabay.com/schools/2010/02/class-size-amendment-moves-forward.html#more**.

Toppo, Greg. "Literacy study: 1 in 7 U.S. adults are unable to read this story," *USA Today*, January 8, 2010, accessed February 9, 2010, **www.usatoday.com/news/education/2009-01-08-adult-literacy_N.htm**.

The United States Department of Education. "President Obama to Announce Plans for 'Race to the Top' Expansion," January 19, 2010, accessed February 19, 2010, **www.whitehouse.gov/the-press-office/ president-obama-announce-plans-race-top-expansion**.

The United States Department of Education. "President's Education Budget Signals Bold Changes for ESEA," February 1, 2010, accessed February 17, 2010, **www2.ed.gov/news/press-releases/2010/02/02012010.html**.

Wagner, Mark. "Yet Another Blog," August 26, 2007, accessed March 9, 2008, **www.decimation.com/markw/2007/08/26/how-to-fire-a-teacher**.

Whale, Robert. "Court: State fails to provide adequate public education," *The Auburn Reporter*, February 17, 2010, accessed February 19, 2010, **www.pnwlocalnews.com/south_king/aub/news/84640582.html**.

Whitaker, Todd. *What Great Principals Do Differently: Fifteen Things That Matter Most*. Larchmont: EYE on Education, 2003.

The White House Office of the Press Secretary. "Remarks by the President on Education," July 24, 2009, accessed February 19, 2010, **www.whitehouse.gov/the_press_office/Remarks-by-the-President-at-the-Department-of-Education/**.

Wohlsletter, Priscilla, and Mohrmon, Susan Albers. "School-Based Management: Strategies for Success," PRE Publications, January 1993, accessed April 12, 2008, **www.ed.gov./pubs/CPRE/fb2sbm.html**.

Zelman, Susan Tave, Superintendent of Public Instruction. "Entry Year Principals and Mentoring Component," June 25, 2007, accessed February 30, 2008, **www.ode.state.oh.us/**.

AUTHOR BIOGRAPHY

With insightful encouragement from her sixth-grade teacher, Tena Green started writing at age 11. In 2000, she took a journalist position for a local newspaper, *The Bellevue Gazette*, where she gained a priceless education from her editor and co-workers. While working for *The Gazette*, she wrote more than 300 articles and started doing freelance work.

Less than two years after starting as a journalist, she published her first novel, *The Catalyst* (2003), and has since written *A Woman's Touch* (2006), *X-30* (2007), a collaboration with friend and horror writer Richard Dean, and *Your First Year as a Principal: Everything You Need to Know That They Don't Teach You in School* (Atlantic Publishing 2009).

Tena continues to write novels, give presentations for students on how to use reading and writing as an outlet, and write books to help educators become effective and successful.

I N D E X